HEINEMANN

TEXT[...]SING

for m[...] awards

WORD PROCESSING AND TYPING EXAM PRACTICE

STAGE II

SHAR[...] [...]ARDS

Heinemann

Heinemann Educational Publishers,
Halley Court, Jordan Hill, Oxford OX2 8EJ
a division of Reed Educational & Professional Publishing Ltd

OXFORD FLORENCE PRAGUE MADRID ATHENS
MELBOURNE AUCKLAND KUALA LUMPUR SINGAPORE TOKYO
IBADAN NAIROBI KAMPALA JOHANNESBURG GABORONE
PORTSMOUTH NH (USA) CHICAGO MEXICO CITY SAO PAULO

First published 1997
2001 2000 99 98
10 9 8 7 6 5 4 3 2 1

A catalogue record for this book is available from the British Library on request.

ISBN 0 435 45387 4

Designed by Jackie Hill

Typeset by TechType, Abingdon, Oxon

Printed and bound in Great Britain by Thomson Litho, Glasgow

Acknowledgements

I would like to thank all those who helped in the preparation of this book, particularly Rosalyn Bass at Heinemann Educational for her advice and encouragement. I would also like to thank my family – Ian, Lucy and Joseph for their help, support and patience while writing this book.

Sharon Spencer

I would like to thank Rosalyn Bass for her help and assistance in the production of this book. I would also like to thank my husband, Arthur, for his endless keying-in, proof-reading and patience.

Barbara Edwards

Contents

About this book

This examination practice book has been written to help you prepare for the Stage II RSA Text Processing Modular Awards in Text Processing, Word Processing and Typewriting. The book is divided into four sections.

1 Preparing for examinations

This section provides you with details of the equipment required for text processing examinations as well as hints and tips on advance preparation and how best to approach examinations. It also provides you with a list of errors which will incur faults in examinations and the opportunity to practise your proof reading skills which should be applied to any work you produce.

The Stage II Word Processing examination requires you to recall previously saved files and make amendments as instructed. The files you will need for the word processing mock examination papers in this book are shown in this section and can be used to practise your keyboarding and accuracy skills.

2 Text Processing

This section provides details of the Text Processing Part 1 examination at Stage II and four mock examination papers to help you prepare for the examination.

3 Word Processing

This section provides details of the Word Processing Part 2 examination at Stage II and four mock examination papers to help you prepare for the examination.

4 Typewriting

This section provides details of the Typewriting Part 2 examination at Stage II and four mock examination papers to help you prepare for the examination.

Format of the book

Some of the tasks in this book may be more demanding than those you will meet in the examinations. This will help you to develop your confidence and ability to succeed in the examinations.

For extra practice, you can work through the exercises in all the sections, even if you are only planning to take one (or two) of the above examinations. This will help you build your speed, increase your accuracy and improve your proof reading skills.

The letterheads, memos and blank pre-printed forms for use with some of the exercises throughout this book can be found at the back of the book.

Worked examples for all the exercises are provided at the back of the book so that you can check your own work. The printed worked examples in this book are reduced by 50 per cent.

Icons

WP This icon represents mock examination papers which have been designed to be undertaken using a word processor. You may also complete these documents for additional typewriting practice.

T This icon represents mock examination papers which have been designed to be undertaken using a typewriter. You may also complete these documents for additional word processing practice.

Section 1

Preparing for examinations

Examinations can be stressful, no matter how well prepared you are. Remembering all the equipment and stationery you will need for the examination will help you remain calm on the day. Make a list of equipment required for word processing and typewriting exams and check this off as you get your things ready.

Check with your centre which of the following it will provide.

- Dictionary.
- Computer or typewriter manual – this can be a software manual or a centre-prepared set of notes. However it must not contain any notes on theory.
- Ruler – showing both inches and millimetres/centimetres.
- Highlighter pen – this is useful for highlighting instructions and amendments to be made.
- Pen – for completing your answer book.
- Pencil – for writing notes such as 'Enc' or a reminder to type a date on your letter or memo.
- Calendar – for inserting dates on letters, memos, etc.
- Correction pen, fluid or papers.

Advance preparation

You should try to eat something before the examination. Although you may not feel like eating beforehand, it will give you the energy to keep going. If you are hungry, you may find you become tired half-way through.

You should of course be on time for your examination. Try to arrive at least 15 minutes before the start time so that you can get organised. There is nothing worse than arriving late and then having to get ready quickly – this will make you feel nervous.

Make sure you understand the centre's instructions for saving your files and printing, etc. Ask questions before the exam starts to clarify these points if necessary.

If it is at all possible, have a five-minute 'warm up'. Type some paragraphs of text to get your fingers moving quickly. This will also help you calm down. Do not worry if you make lots of mistakes at this point.

During the examination

Try to have your strategy planned before the exam begins. It is helpful if you start with a short and comparatively easy task. It is not usually a good idea to start with the task containing a table. It can take a few minutes to get into the exam and so a simple task will build your confidence and help you relax. Use the time schedules given in each section of this book to see how long you should spend on each task.

You should allow around five minutes of examination time to read the instructions carefully. It is often helpful to highlight the instructions with a highlighter pen before you start a task. This will act as a checklist and you will be able to tick off the instructions as you carry them out. Make a pencil note on the exam paper to remind you of enclosures or dates that need to be inserted. Do not forget to check the examination paper carefully – you may often find instructions dotted around the page.

If you do make a mistake, try not to start the task again unless absolutely necessary. Do not forget that errors such as not leaving a space between words or forgetting to indicate a new paragraph will incur only one fault. If you start the task again and then fail to complete it, you will incur many more faults.

Remember that if you attempt each task you stand a chance of passing the exam. However, if there is a task missing, you will automatically fail. This means you must check that all tasks are clearly labelled and included in your answer book.

In your time plan allow at least ten minutes for checking your work carefully. This is probably the most important part of the examination. If you are using a word processor, one approach is to key in all the tasks and when you have finished, run each task through the spell check. This will pick up any typographical or basic spelling errors. Then, spend any time remaining checking each piece of work carefully in case you have left out a sentence or failed to carry out an instruction. Check that you have numbered any continuation pages, that you have the required number of copies and that you have used the correct stationery.

If your centre allows you to print your work during the examination, then do take advantage of this if time allows. It is often much easier to proof read printed work than check from the screen. If you are limited to the amount of paper you can use, do not forget you can print on the back of your sheets of paper. Although this is not ideal, you will only incur one fault and it is much better than not handing in a task.

If you are using a typewriter, check your work whilst it is still in the machine as it is easier to line up to correct.

Do not forget to type your full name, centre number and task number on each sheet of paper. You should complete your answer book very carefully, paying particular attention to writing your name clearly. This is where the examining board will get the information that appears on your certificate, so make sure your name is spelt correctly and is easy to read.

Good luck!

Proof reading skills

One of the most common reasons for candidates to fail examinations is their failure to proof read properly. Once you have finished typing a piece of work, you must read it through very carefully, checking it word for word against the examination paper.

This section aims to help you improve your proof reading skills by showing you the type of errors that are commonly made in examinations. Test yourself by finding the errors in the proof reading exercises and then check them against the keys at the back of the book. These will help you develop good proof reading skills and will point out where candidates often go wrong in examinations.

Typographical and spelling errors

Typographical errors are common typing mistakes such as transposing letters within a word. For example 'hte' instead of 'the'. They are different from spelling errors and do not relate to how well a person can spell. Other examples of typographical errors include

- not having a capital letter at the beginning of a sentence (poor use of the shift key)
- not leaving a space between words (failing to hit the space bar hard enough)
- too many spaces between words or spaces within words (hitting the space bar too hard)
- additional characters within a word (pressing a key too hard or leaving your finger on a key for too long)
- omission of a character(s) within a word (pressing the key too lightly)
- capital letters within words (hitting the shift key by mistake)
- incorrect letters used (having your fingers on the wrong keys to start with)
- transposing letters (trying to type too quickly)
- numbers appearing within words (having your fingers in the wrong place).

If you notice many typographical errors in your work, it may be helpful to revise the keyboard and improve your typing technique. You do not need to go back to the beginning, just practise some typing drills each time you start to type. You only need to spend a few minutes each day on drills and you will soon notice the difference. The work you produce should become much more accurate and your typing speeds will increase.

If you are typing too quickly and are making many mistakes, then slow down a little. In the long run your work will be completed much more quickly if you do not have to go back to correct mistakes.

Proof Reading Practice Exercise 1

WP **T** Look at the paragraph below and see how many typographical errors you can find.

If you are a student at a Colelge of Further Education, then don't forget to join th e Students' Union. it can give you lots of benefits. By having a student Union card you may be able to get discount on many items. Tehse include stationery, meals, drinks, tickets for the thea4tre or cinema. YOu can also purcahse a Student Travel Card which entitles you to discount on train and caoch fares.

Your Student Union may also arrange events such as discos, rag week or charity events. These can begreat fun and are a useful way of getting to know students fro m other courses.

■ Spelling errors and errors of agreement

If you know that spelling is not one of your strengths, then you must check your work extra carefully. Unless a word has been circled as being incorrect, then you can copy the words from the examination paper knowing that they are correct. You will, however, have to learn all the abbreviations and how to spell them in full.

Once you have completed a piece of work, use the spell check facility, if you have one. This will help you to pick up any typographical errors and any obvious spelling mistakes. If there are any words that are questioned, then check carefully to ensure you choose the correct alternative. This is particularly important if your spell check uses an American dictionary. If you are unsure, then use an English dictionary. You must also check that you have typed the correct word if there are two meanings, for example, their and there.

Errors of agreement are always circled for you to correct, for example, 'We *was* going to have a picnic' instead of 'We *were* going to have a picnic'.

Proof Reading Practice Exercise 2

WP **T** Look at the paragraph below. How many spelling mistakes can you find?

It was agred at the recent Bored meeting that the company should employ a number of temporery staff to asist with the proposed office move. The move will take place at the end of next month. It will give the company the opportunitey to expand its buisiness and therfore become more profitible.

The Board would like to congratulate staff on increesed productevity in recent monthes. This effort will be reflected in the company's acounts which will be published next week. A bones of 3% will be paid to staff in their next salry payment.

■ Layout errors

There are many different layout errors that can be made. They include the following.

- Failure to date letters, memos and pre-printed forms.
- Left-hand or top margins of less than 13 mm (1/2 inch) or a ragged left-hand margin.
- No clear line space before and after separate items.
- Failure to start a new paragraph as instructed in the draft.
- Inconsistent spacing between paragraphs.
- Inconsistent use of time, money, weights, spellings, punctuation, words and figures within a document.
- Incorrect emphasis of words or sentences.
- Use of line spacing not as instructed.
- Incorrect use of stationery.
- Headings, references, etc. not as shown in the draft.
- Incorrect centring.
- Initial capitals used incorrectly – either added or omitted.
- Failure to range whole numbers or text in columns.
- Insetting of text carried out incorrectly.
- Failure to justify text as instructed.
- Incorrect adjustment of line length.
- Failure to number continuation sheets.

- Failure to indicate an enclosure(s).
- Failure to rule lines correctly (typewriting examinations).
- Failure to use the same coloured ink for drawing table lines (typewriting examinations).
- Failure to leave clear spaces above and below, right and left of lines (typewriting examinations).
- Failure to produce extra copies.
- Failure to indicate routing of extra copies.
- Failure to allocate correct amount of space as instructed in the draft.

These faults are less common than accuracy errors, but you will need to check your work carefully against the examination paper to ensure that you avoid making any of them. If you are using a word processor and can print during the examination, then you should do so. It is much easier to proof read a 'hard copy' than to check work on the screen. If you are not able to print out your work, then use the 'print review' facility so that you can see how your work looks before it is printed.

Proof Reading Practice Exercise 3

WP **T**

In the following document there are three layout errors and five typographical errors. When you have found them, type a correct copy of the document and check your proof reading skills with the key and error sheet shown at the back of the book.

The Saxo Phones

this five-piece jazz band has just embarked on a nationwide tour. It will be playing at many venues throughout the country.

The Saxo Phones have a reputation for being a great live act.Their music is guaranteed to make you swing.

Given below are some of the dates it will be playing in this area.

Bath	1 April
Bristol	3 April
Cheltnham	21 April
Swindon	4 May
Yeovil	26 May
Chippenham	27 May

Full details can be obtained from your local music store.   Look out for advertisements in the local newSpaper. Tickets can be purchasedin advance for all venues.

Come and swing with The Saxo Phones!

Proof Reading Practice Exercise 4

WP **T**

In the following document there are six layout errors and three spelling errors. When you have found them, type a correct copy of the letter and check your proof reading skills with the key and error sheet shown at the back of the book.

1

THE TOY
CHEST

38 Helston Street
YORK
YO27 2NV

Phone 018392 238283
Fax 018392 376762

Our ref SL/MA/62

8 August 1997

FOR THE ATTENTION OF

Mr Stuart Lovell
Lovell Direct Marketing
9 Penn Lea Avenue
Milton Keynes
MK43 8BT
Dear Mr Lovell

Thank you for your recent letter setting out your terms of buisness.

I have now had the opportunity to discuss your terms with my collegues. I am pleased to inform you that we would like to purchase additional names and addresses for our mailing lists.

As you are aware, we are a toy company specialising in high quality, educational toys. We would be interested in purchasing the names of those who have young children in the age range of 1-twelve years.

  Please prepare a mailing list of 10,000 names and addresses in the format given on the attached specification. If possible, we would like to include these in our next mailing. This is due to go out on 12 September.

Please do not hesitate to contact me if you require any further iformation.

Yours sincerely

Mandy Atkins
Mail Order Manager

Proof Reading Practice Exercise 5

WP **T**

Compare the following two documents. You should find ten mistakes in the second document. When you have finished, type a correct version of the document and check your proof reading skills with the key and error sheet shown at the back of the book.

Document 1

China and Glassware Department

We are having a clearance sale next week. The table below shows the ranges that are being discounted together with the sale prices. Please ensure that the prices have been changed before the sale begins on Monday.

When customers purchase these items it should be pointed out that these ranges have been discontinued.

Item	Code No	Price £	Sale Price £
<u>Alice Range</u>			
Dinner plate	AL9	5.50	4.00
Cereal bowl	AL3	4.80	3.60
Cup and saucer	AL8	8.90	7.50
Side plate	AL10	4.50	3.00
Serving plate	AL12	25.00	18.00
<u>Tessa Range</u>			
Teapot	TE20	35.00	27.50
Sugar bowl	TE25	10.50	8.00
Milk jug	TE23	12.50	9.50
Salad bowl	TE16	25.00	22.00
Butter dish	TE19	15.00	10.00
<u>Crystal Range</u>			
Large wine glass	CR41	6.00	4.00
Small wine glass	CR48	5.00	3.50
Champagne flute	CR31	8.00	5.50
Whisky tumbler	CR44	4.50	3.00
Liqueur glass	CR36	5.00	3.50

Document 2

China and Glassware Department

We are having a clearance sale next week. The table below shows the ranges that are being discounted together with the sale prices.

Please ensure that the prices have been changed before the sale begins on Monday.

When customers purchase these items it should be pointed out that these ranges have been discontinued.

Item	Price £	Code No	Sale Price £
<u>Alice Range</u>			
Dinner plate	5.50	AL9	4.00
Cereal bowl	4.80	AL3	3.60
Cup and saucer	8.90	AL8	7.50
Side plate	4.50	AL10	3.00
Serving plate	25.00	AL12	18.00
Crystal Range			
Large wine glass	6.00	CR41	4.00
Small wine glass	5.00	CR48	3.50
Champagne flute	8.00	CR31	5.50
Whisky tumbler	4.50	CR45	3.00
Liqueur glass	5.00	CR36	3.50
<u>Tessa Range</u>			
Teapot	TE20	35.00	27.50
Sugar bowl	TE25	10.50	8.00
Milk jug	TE23	12.50	9.50
Salad bowl	TE16	25.00	22.00
Butter dish	TE19	15.00	12.00

Additional text

During the Stage II Text Processing examination you will be handed an extra section for inclusion in one of the documents. Please ensure you remember to insert the extra section where instructed. The extra sections for the text processing mock examination papers in this book are shown on the following pages.

WP T

Additional text Exam Practice 1 Document 3

typist/operator: this is the extra section for Document 3

Do not use chemicals but try organic methods instead. Start a compost heap or use a compost bin.

Plant trees if you have room as they help to absorb excess carbon-dioxide. Do not burn anything other than woody garden waste on a bonfire.

WP T

Additional text Exam Practice 2 Document 3

Commission

As agreed in our contract, the Gallery will take 20% Commission on all sales. Although this may seem rather high, we would point out that this includes the cost of staffing the Gallery, the private View, Cat and all publicity.

Any orders or commissions accepted though introductions made at the Gallery are also subject to a 20% fee.

Operator/Typist: this is the extra section for Document 3.

Max Hanson

Clocks of all types and sizes are Max's speciality. Max has been making clocks for many yrs and uses a variety of materials. These beautiful timepieces will become heirlooms to be ~~cherished through~~ handed down the generations.

Nicholas Millard

The wonderful range of pottery Nicholas produces are modern and colourful. Each item is sold seperately so you can start yr collection straightaway.

His work is fun and practical.

Operator: These are the extra paragraphs for document 3.

WP T

Additional text Exam Practice 4 Document 3

typist/operator: this is the extra paragraph for Document 3

You will be within a few minutes' walk of the Roman Baths, the perfect place to take your guests when they come to visit you. The therapeutic value of the spa still remains today. Alongside the baths is the Pump Room. Afternoon tea here is a must.

Recalled text

The Stage II Word Processing examination requires you to recall previously saved files and phrases and make amendments as instructed. The files and phrases you will need for the word processing mock examination papers in this book should be typed exactly as shown in the draft documents which follow (except for line endings and any page breaks, which must be allowed to occur naturally). Some of the documents require you to key in text with deliberate errors for you to correct when the files are recalled – these are circled. To undertake these mock papers under exam conditions, key in the passages as shown (including the errors). When undertaking the mock examination papers you will be instructed to correct the errors.

Save the files under the file name given but do not print a copy.

In the examination, these documents will be keyed in by your tutor in advance. However, when working through this book, use these documents to practise your keyboarding and accuracy skills.

Recalled text Exam Practice 1 Document 1

WP

> Instruction: Key in the following text exactly as shown (except for line endings and any page break which must be allowed to occur naturally). Use single-line spacing and a ragged right-hand margin. Use a line length of (a) 15.5 cm or (b) 60 characters. If proportional spacing is used, please ensure a line length of (a). Save as DECOR1.

HOME DECORATION

If you are looking to brighten up your house why not try some different paint effects. These are quick, easy and inexpensive but can make a great difference to your home. You do not have to be a talented artist as these effects are easy to do.

Colourwashing - This has a subtle effect which adds tone and colour. It is good for covering uneven plasterwork. This may be useful if you live in an old property.

When this coat has dried, you will be able to see if there are any areas that are uneven. Try to make the strokes cross the first coat strokes at right angles.

Apply two base coats of emulsion paint with a roller. Allow to dry thoroughly. When dry, apply a coat of colourwash using criss cross strokes. Vary the angle of the strokes to show the base coat underneath.

Stencilling - This is simple to do but very effective. Stencil kits containing paints, brushes and stencils are available at art shops and DIY stores. If you are more adventurous you can easily make your own designs using strong card or acetate.

Stippling - To achieve this effect you paint a layer of glaze over your base colour. Then using a stipple brush, you break up the colour into a series of dots which when dry gives a texture rather like airbrushing.

Apply two coats of base colour using eggshell paint. When this has dried you can apply the glaze in strips. Now using a stipple brush dipped in colour, stab the wall at right angles so that the colour breaks up into the glaze. If you are using this effect in a kitchen or bathroom, you may need to apply a coat of clear varnish.

When this has dried, follow these steps again using a toning colour.

Sponging - This gives a mottled effect and can look very attractive. You will need a small sea sponge to achieve this effect.

After applying two coats of base colour, allow to dry thoroughly. Pour a little paint in a tray and dab the sponge in. Squeeze the sponge gently to remove excess paint. Now, dab the wall with the sponge in a random direction. Change the direction of the sponge occasionally to get a speckled effect.

There are many good books for sale which give full details of these techniques. Your local DIY store may also offer help and advice.

There are also a number of courses and workshops available. Find out if your local college has any courses on offer.

Recalled text Exam Practice 1 Document 2

WP

Instruction: Key in the following text exactly as shown. Save as DECOR2.

Colourwashing
Stippling
Marbling
Rag rolling
Stencilling
Sponging

Recalled text Exam Practice 1 Document 4

WP

Instruction: Key in the following phrases and save as shown. Do not key in the phrase numbers as part of the recalled text – they are shown for identification purposes only.

Phrase 1 (save as DECOR3)

Studio 15

Phrase 2 (save as DECOR4)

Sponging

Phrase 3 (save as DECOR5)

Stencilling

Recalled text Exam Practice 2 Document 1

WP

Instruction: Key in the following text exactly as shown (except for paragraph line endings and any page break which must be allowed to occur naturally). Use single-line spacing and a ragged right-hand margin. Ensure a line length of either (a) 14 cm or (b) 55 characters. If proportional spacing is used, please ensure a line length of (a). Circled text indicates a deliberate error which must be typed as shown (do not correct error). Save as CARAVAN1.

Touring Caravan Holidays

Firstly check your caravan tyre pressures, and wheel-nut tightness. Turn off the gas cylinder and make sure it is strapped upright.

Before you start your holiday you must ensure your van has been serviced regularly so that it is safe in all respects when touring on the road and on site. It is a good idea to have this done early in the year before your first trip.

Empty all liquid containers and carry any water required for your journey in a small container in the car. Secure any loose items in the van, close windows and rooflights. Fasten travel catch on cupboards and refrigerator.

Many people now wear gloves to protect their hands when doing these outdoor chores.

You can now hitch your caravan on to your towing vehicle. Wind the jockey wheel down. Clamp the jockey wheel securely in place and fit stabiliser if used.

If you are going to use a trailer tent as a cooking area it is wise to have a large bucket of water handy when sited. This is in addition to the fire extinguisher and fire blanket. It is always wise to be prepared.

There are a number of safety devices you can carry you carry a 1 kg dry powder extinguisher. A fire blanket is advisable for the kitchen area and also a smoke detector.

The noseweight of the caravan will have to be checked. The recommended figure will be in your handbook. Ensure your handbrake is fully on and then raise corner steadies and stow winding handle and step.
Lock the door.

On arrival at your site check in first with the owner or warden. Be sure to follow instructions given by them for siting your caravan. In order to make sure your refrigerator operates properly level the caravan to within 3 degrees. After you are safely settled on a pitch fit the hitchlock and wheel clamp to secure your caravan. You now deserve that welcome cup of tea!

Recalled text Exam Practice 2 Document 2

WP

> Instruction: Key in exactly as shown (except for paragraph line endings, which must be allowed to occur naturally). Save as CARAVAN2.

CARAVAN INSURANCE COVER

We can arrange insurance cover for your caravan, your car or motor caravan. Our premiums are very favourable and we can provide the insurance you personally need.

If you travel abroad in Europe we can provide free foreign travel cover provided your journey does not exceed 31 days. For motor caravan drivers up to 3 months cover is provided. Special arrangements can be made for longer periods.

Our motor caravan foreign travel covers the following.

Awnings
Aerials
Baggage
Batteries
Heaters
Radios
Cassette players
Toilet tents
Water carriers
Television

Our most popular insurance choice includes comprehensive cover on or off the road.

Recalled text Exam Practice 2 Document 4

WP

> Instruction: Key in the following phrases and save as shown. Do not key in the phrase numbers as part of the recalled text – they are shown for identification purposes only.

Phrase 1 (save as CARAVAN3)

You have worked as deputy wardens for a number of years and this will be your first post in charge of a site.

Phrase 2 (save as CARAVAN4)

A full list of duties and responsibilities for the post will be sent to you on receipt of your acceptance.

Phrase 3 (save as CARAVAN5)

Your post will commence on 1 March and end on 31 October and the site is open to caravaners from 31 March to 3 October.

Recalled text Exam Practice 3 Document 1

WP

> Instruction: Key in the following text exactly as shown (except for line endings and any page break, which must be allowed to occur naturally). Use single-line spacing and a ragged right-hand margin. Ensure a line length of either (a) 15.5 cm or (b) 60 characters. If proportional spacing is used, please ensure a line length of (a). Save as HOMES1.

Cornwall's Finest Holiday Homes

This leaflet aims to tell you about our booking agency and to give you information on how to turn your holiday home into a successful business.

We are a long-established booking agency concentrating on homes in Cornwall. Each year we produce a full-colour brochure featuring over 350 homes to let.

Our experience in this business means that we can give an expert opinion as to the potential of your holiday property. We can also advise you on the amount of rent you can realistically expect to receive.

The full-colour brochure features a photograph of every property together with professionally written details. We receive over 45,000 enquiries each year.

By choosing us as your booking agent you can be assured you will receive a first-class service. Our competent staff deal with all the details on your behalf. They provide a friendly and efficient service. Our offices are open from 9.30 am to 6.30 pm seven days a week. This means you will never miss an opportunity for letting your home.

The Tourist Board has an inspection service that grades holiday properties on a scale of 1 to 5. This is assessed on a yearly basis and offers peace of mind to our customers. The assessment gives helpful feedback on making the most of your property. We do not accept properties that have a grading of less than 4.

We advise our property owners to take out cancellation insurance. This can be arranged through our offices. This means that should a holiday be cancelled because of accident or ill-health, etc, you will receive 85% of the usual price. You will also require Public Liability insurance for your property. It is advised that you insure your home and contents against accidental damage by customers. Our agency has arranged a special deal with a local insurance company. It can offer you very reasonable rates for this service. Please let us know if you would like further details.

You will probably wish to take some weeks for your friends and family. We ask you to limit this to four during the year. A maximum of two can be taken during the peak season. You do not have to let your home for the entire year. The minimum number of weeks is 24. A short break offer for the winter months is very popular with our customers. You may wish to consider this for your property.

As we deal with many properties our commission charges are extremely reasonable. A basic rate of 15% plus VAT is payable for each booking. A yearly charge of £75 is also payable for the Tourist Board inspection.

Recalled text Exam Practice 3 Document 2

WP

Instruction: Key in the following text exactly as shown. Save as HOMES2.

After the property has been inspected a full and detailed report will be written. This feedback is extremely useful in helping owners upgrade their homes.

Recalled text Exam Practice 3 Document 4

WP

Instruction: Key in the following phrases and save as shown. Do not key in the phrase numbers as part of the recalled text – they are shown for identification purposes only.

Phrase 1 (save as HOMES3)

Grade One

Phrase 2 (save as HOMES4)

£340 per week

Phrase 3 (save as HOMES5)

Grade Four

Recalled text Exam Practice 4 Document 1

WP

Key in the following text exactly as shown (except for line endings and any page break which must be allowed to occur naturally). Use single-line spacing and a ragged right-hand margin. Ensure a line length of either (a) 15.5 cm or (b) 60 characters. If proportional spacing is used, please ensure a line length of (a). Circled text indicates a deliberate error which must be typed as shown (do not correct error). Save as GARDEN1.

A Garden For Wildlife

No matter how small your garden, it can be a paradise for birds and other wildlife. A small pond is imperative as it makes a home for frogs and insects. It is also a place for birds to drink and bathe.

Plant a few shrubs that have berries as these make natural food for birds. They also give winter food for all kinds of small creatures.

Although a Bhuddleia shrub can grow quite tall its blooms attract many different butterflies.

Blackbirds and thrushes find a lawn a perfect feeding ground. No matter how small your garden is birds will be frequent visitors. You cannot fail to see him with his bright orange-red face and breast.

Build the pond with gently sloping sides. Have a stone wall close by for shelter for the frogs and toads.

Keep those precious autumn leaves and pile them under shrubs and hedges. Fill hedge hog boxes with them and put some in bin liners to rot down for use next year. You are likely to find a wren poking among ground litter and picking food from the leaves. The wren has a tiny body but a loud voice, listen for its fast and shrill song. You will be surprised how much noise it can make.

Listen for spring being heralded at both dawn and dusk by the blackbird's song.

These birds are perhaps our commonest of garden birds and nest in bushes.

From September think about bird food holders. Small birds have to eat all day to survive the cold winter nights. The blue tit has very acrobatic feeding habits. Watch him feeding on a nut holder.

If you are keen on gardens and wildlife visit our organic gardens, send for our free booklet listing these. Our gardens are at their best in the summer. The best time to visit is June and July.

Put your bird table and feeders near to plants that climb or a shrub to give the birds shelter. Although you may not fancy a bath outside at this time of year, it is important for birds to have one. They bathe to keep their feathers in good condition. Replace frozen water in a bird bath each morning or float a ball in your pond to keep a small patch ice-free.

Recalled text Exam Practice 4 Document 2

WP

> Instruction: Key in exactly as shown (except for paragraph line endings, which must be allowed to occur naturally). Save as GARDEN2.

A POOL IN YOUR GARDEN

Water can be delightful in a garden. Its sight and sound are both relaxing and refreshing. The shape and size of a pool will depend on the site chosen for it. A generous rectangular, circular or oval shape is the most effective. If you have a large garden a more irregular shape to form part of the natural landscape would be more in character.

The design course dates are as follows.

10 September 1997
6 September 1997
8 October 1997
13 September 1997
18 October 1997
27 September 1997

The design course will begin with coffee and registration at 10.30 am.

Recalled text Exam Practice 4 Document 4

WP

> Instruction: Key in the following phrases and save as shown. Do not key in the phrase numbers as part of the recalled text – they are shown for identification purposes only.

Phrase 1 (save as GARDEN3)

We will accept cancellations from students up to 2 weeks before the date of the course. They will not be entitled for a refund of fees.

Phrase 2 (save as GARDEN4)

Please ensure you have enough materials you will all respectively need for the courses. We have always had a high standard of efficiency and would like to maintain this.

Phrase 3 (save as GARDEN5)

On 26 October the tree course will be held in room 4 as room 3 is being decorated that weekend. Students will be informed of this change at registration.

Text Processing

The Stage II Text Processing Part 1 examination offered by RSA Examinations Board tests your ability to key in and lay out three business documents. You may use either a typewriter or word processor to complete the examination.

You will be asked to type three documents in one and a quarter hours. These are

- a letter
- a memo
- a report or article.

One of the documents will require a continuation sheet – ensure the continuation sheet is numbered.

In order to pass the examination you must complete the paper within the time given and incur no more than 11 faults. If you incur only 4 faults or less, you will be awarded a distinction.

The tasks will contain corrections and amendments for you to make. Words that need correcting will be circled. These include spelling errors, punctuation and errors of agreement.

Make sure you are familiar with the RSA list of abbreviations and spelling for Stage II.

Ensure the correct stationery is used. Letters must be produced on letterheads and memos on memo paper. Your centre may provide you with pre-printed paper or a template on a word processor. Remember to date letters and memos with the date of the examination, include special marks as instructed and an enclosure mark if appropriate. Ensure you leave a clear line space after the printed headings before you start typing.

The letterheads and pre-printed memo forms for use with the text processing mock examination papers which follow can be found at the back of the book.

During the examination you will be handed an extra section for inclusion in one of the documents. Please ensure you remember to insert the extra section where instructed. The extra sections for the text processing mock examination papers in this book can be found on pages 11–13.

You will be asked to check a detail from one task for insertion in another. Check this very carefully.

One problem candidates face is running out of time in the examination. Not only must you complete the examination paper but you should also have enough time left to check your work carefully. When you are working through the mock examination papers in this section, you may like to make a note of the time each document has taken. As a guide you should aim to complete the tasks within the following time scale.

- Letter – 15 minutes.
- Memo – 15 minutes.
- Report or article – 30 minutes.

This will allow you a total of 15 minutes to read the instructions before you type and to check through your work on completion.

Exam Practice 1 Document 1

WP **T**

2

Our ref PW|CE

Mighty Trees
Poplar Business Park
YORK
YO2 5JR

Mark this FOR THE ATTENTION OF MR EDWARD JENKINS

Dr Sirs

Thank you for your letter expressing interest in the conference we plan to run next year on the enviroment. I has noted that you will be willing to speak on trees and woodland issues in general. ~~I will contact you again in the near future~~.

Would you please ensure yr talk gives information on our traditional trees. Oak, beech, hazel and ash should be included. You may wish to expand your talk on one of these species, for example the oak, explaining that it is one of our richest of natural habitats. Many birds ~~five~~ nest in the oak. ✓ Wasps can lay eggs in young acorns. Butterflies' can live high in the oak canopy.

We need to stress that our anceint woods and heritage are worth conserving, the vanous raesons why our woods have been destroyed and what the new challenges we face are. All this will make very interesting info for our delegates to here.

I will be in touch with you again in the near future.

Yrs ffly

Paul Waterson
Conference Secretary

Exam Practice 1 Document 2

WP T

Memo

From Paul Waterson

To Janet Parks

Ref PW|CE

We are getting a very good response from potential speaker for our conference on the environment I attach a list of the replies received so far.

We need to analyse the list and ensure we have a good coverage of all aspects to do with the environment. // When we have done this we will have the opp to contact cos we feel are still needed to give us a balanced conference.

It may be nec for us to conttact specialist speakers' for certain areas. I will keep you informed of how things are progressing on a weekly basis.

So far we have had no response from anyone to talk about the ozone layer.

Exam Practice 1 Document 3

WP **T**

Typist/operator: the extra section for this document can be found on page 11.

2

single linespacing except where indicated

SUBJECTS FOR CONFERENCE ON THE ENVIRONMENT

some

We have had confirmation from speakers who is willing to talk on the following subjects.

We need

~~I should like~~ to have a complete draft of the conference by (give date for first Monday of next month).

<u>Recycling</u>

Make use of the many collection points for metals, glass, paper, and other materials.

Make your own compost from garden waist.

Recycling reduces the waste of raw materails and less energy is needed to produce new goods. Many authorities have prepared recycling plans.

A lot of our household waste is buried on land. About half of this could be usefully recycled.

<u>In the home</u>

As well as saving you ~~money~~ lessen

~~You can help yourself save some cash~~, you can help ~~towards~~ the threat of acid rain and global climate change by using energy more effficiently in the home.

Insulate your walls and fit thick loft insulation Ensure all doors and windows are draught proof. Turn off all unused lights and appliances, especially televisions.

<u>In the garden</u>

Private gardens are important for providing foood, water and shelter for birds and some wildlife. typist/operator: insert extra section here

On the road

All forms of transport

~~Cars and lorries~~ cause air pollution through exhaust fumes. Use unleaded petrol if your car can take it. Take a/c of fuel economy and drive smoothly.

Walk, cycle or use public transport whenever you can. even when a bus is only a quarter full it is twice as fuel efficient as a family car.

Noise

Noise can cause severe stress. Never under-estimate the harmful effects of noise. It is the form of pollution which has the most immediate effect on people.

Trees and woodland issues (these paragraphs only in double linespacing)

Trees produce oxygen, influence our weather and prevent soil erosion. They help to filter dust, smoke and fumes within our towns and cities.

You can help us in the fight against pollusion by planting more trees in your garden.

Join an org ~~who~~ which are interested in preserving and building up our woodlands.

In the countryside

Always observe the country code and close gates, ~~keep to~~ stay on public footpaths, and keep dogs under control. Do not pick or uproot any wild plants. Remember that wild plants and endangered animals are protected by law. There are over 160 species of plants protected under law.

Rivers, lakes, beaches and drinking water

Pollutants get into water through the drains and other discharges. Never put any left-over chemicals down the drain, toilet or in a stream.

We still need speakers on the greenhouse effect, and the o____ l_____.

Exam Practice 2 Document 1

WP **T**

Our ref RF/EH1/PB

Mr Robert Frost
3A Dunsford Pl
IPSWICH
Suffolk
IP39 1QQ

Dr Robert

I am ~~delighted~~ pleased to inform you that the plans for your forthcoming exhibition at the Aqua Art Gallery (is) now taking shape. // As (discused), the exhibition will run for three weeks beg on Friday 20 September. You will be (expeted) to provide the exhibits one week in advance. This will allow plenty of time for setting up the exhibition.

A private (veiwing) has been arranged for the Friday evening. This will take place [in the Gallery] from 7.00 pm to 2030 hours. Wine and canapes will be served. Please let my sec ~~know~~ have the names and addresses of those you would like to invite. Please limit the no of guests to 20.

I am enclosing a sheet giving further details of our terms and conditions.

We look forward to a very (sucessful) partnership with you.

Yrs sncly

Patrick Beresford
Manager

Exam Practice 2 Document 2

WP **T**

Memo

Please mark this URGENT

From Patrick Beresford
To Faye Woods
Ref PB/FW/RFEH1

The dates of Robert Frosts' exhibition have now been finalised. The private view has been arranged for F_____ – _____. This will take place from 7.00pm to 8.30pm.

As usual, wine and canapes will be served. I would be grateful if you could arrange for 3 local catering company's to provide some quotations.

I believe there will be approx 150 people attending this event. The food and wine must be of good quality. A budget of around £3.50 per head has been set. However this figure may have to be increased. ~~We could go up to £4.50 per head.~~

The invitasions will need to be printed soon. Please arrange for these to be designed. You will need to check with Toby as I beleve he has the front cover design. // Robert Frost will be letting you have a list of his guests. I have asked him to limit this to 20 people. You should have in your files a list of the guests ~~that~~ who are usually invited to ~~the~~ private viewings. Please check this is up to date and amend if necy.

already completed

Exam Practice 2 Document 3

WP T

Typist/operator: the extra section for this document can be found on page 11.

Use single line-spacing except where indicated

A Guide for Exhibitors

Emphasise this heading

Holding an exhibition is a very exicting time. However it can also be rather stressful. The success of the exhibition depends largely on its org. We aim to provide all the back-up required to make your exhbition as stressfree and successful as possible. In order for us to provide this service, we need you to be aware of the following:

Layout

Our staff are very experinced in setting out exhibitions to their best advantage. Exhibitors are very welcome to come and view the setting up of their work. ~~Yr suggestions are always welcome~~. However, we would respectfully remind you that the contract gives us full control of the exhibition layout.

Deadlines

Whilst we ~~appreciate~~ realise it can be difficult to keep to deadlines they are very necy to the smooth running of the exhibition. Please ensure that your work reaches the Gallery by the agreed date. In order to make the most of your work, our staff need to have several days to plan the exhibition fully. If you donot provide yr work on time, then an extra charge of 1% ~~of~~ on all sales will be levied.

* Insert extra paragraphs here.

Catalogue

A full-colour cat will be prepared on behalf of the Gallery. This will be produced at the Gallerys' exp. The design, copy and layout will be controlled by the Gallery. The copyright will be assigned to Aqua Art Gallery. In order to ensure that the information given is completely accurate, it will be the resp of the artist to check the copy.

This paragraph only in double line-spacing

Pricing

It is hoped that the price of the exhibits will be agreed between the exhibitor and the Gallery. The Gallery has a great deal of exp in this area and can give realistic advice.

Private View

This is a very important ocasion as art critics, dealers and buyers attend. Please ensure you are available for this event and are prepared to be interviewed by the press.

Payment

Payment for work sold will be made by cheque no later than 28 days after the closing date of the exhibition. Any comission fees will be deducted before payment is made.

We hope that your exhibition is very successful.

Exam Practice 3 Document 1

WP **T**

Our ref EV/PM/192

Ms Ella Vaughan
Rose Cottage
DRUIDSTONE
Pembs
PB82 3NE

Dr Ms Vaughan

Thank you for your recent letter and photographs of yr craft work. I have now had the opp to (discuss) yr work with my (collegues). We believe we will be able to sell yr ~~work~~ jewellery through our craft shop.// I would be grateful if you could make an appointment to see me. May I suggest Thursday of next week, (Operator: give date). Please ring my assistant, Josie Walters to arrange a convenient time.

If yr work is (acepted) we would expect you to be able to keep yr area fully stocked through out the yr.// A commission of 30% is taken from all sales of yr work to cover the shop overheads. Orders for work taken through the shop (is) also subject to the commission payment.

I look forward to meeting you.

Yrs sncly

Peter Marshall
Manager

Please bring samples of yr jewellery.

Exam Practice 3 Document 2

WP **T**

Memo

Please mark this URGENT

From Peter Marshall

To Josie Walters

Ref JW/PM/EV

I am enclosing a copy of a letter from E——— V———, together with some photographs of her work. I (beleve) the jewellery is just what we are looking for to fill the space we have now Graham has left.

As you will see, I have asked Ms Vaughan to contact you to make an appointment. I can meet her at any time on Thursday.

Last week I left you a leaflet to type and have printed. Have you been able to do ~~anything with~~ this yet? I would be (gratefull) if you could make this a priority.

We need to have the leaflet ready for the ~~start~~ beginning of the (✓) tourist season. Please let me have a draft copy to check before you take it to the printers. We should have approx 500 printed to start with. Please telephone three printers to find out the cost.

Exam Practice 3 Document 3

WP **T**

Typist/operator: the extra section for this document can be found on page 12.

Use single line-spacing except where indicated.

Craft Fayre ← Emphasise this heading

Craft Fayre sells hand-made goods made by local craftspeople. The shop is ideally placed for the tourist trade and is building a reputation amongst local people for it's unusual and beautiful gifts.

There is a large range of gifts on ~~display~~ sale including jewellery, hand-knitted garments, ceramics, clocks, paintings and silk scarves. The Craft Fayre is always searching for new and interesting items. This means the range changes regularly.

This paragraph only in double line-spacing

Among the regular contributors to the Craft Fayre are:

Katy Medworth

Samantha is a watercolour expert. Her paintings of local places of interest and landscapes are very popular. She has exhibited at many galleries throughout the country and studied at St Martin's School of Art.

Samantha Jacobs

Katy is a silk screen printer. On sale at the Craft Fayre is a range of her silk scarves and greeting cards. The limited edition designs for her silk scarves are both unusual and eye-catching. The range of greeting cards is suitable for any ocassion.

Ryan Dolman

Mirrors and picture frames are Ryan's speciality. They are hand-painted with bright, modern designs. If you have a particular design in mind, Ryan will be delighted to make a frame to yr own specification. These make excellent gifts.

Ricky Thompson

Ricky makes the most exquisite leather goods. Handbags, belts, purses and briefcases form his range. The designs are unique and the goods are beautifully made. Only the best quality leather is used.

Mary Lovell

Hand-knitted garments in every colour and style can be found in Mary's display of goods. A variety of yarns are used including cashmere wool, cotton and silks.

Operator: Insert the extra paragraphs here.

Oliver Sinclair

Hand-crafted furniture made from pine is Olivers' trade. A small range of cupboards and chairs can be seen at the Craft Fayre. Larger pieces such as wardrobes, beds and dressers can be seen at Oliver's workshop.

Freya Andrews

Freya designs and makes clothes especially for young children. They are made in 100% cotton and are easy to wash. Children love th4e bright colours and modern designs. At very reasonable prices, these are always popular with our customers.

We look forward to seeing you soon.

Exam Practice 4 Document 1

WP T

Our ref JE/398

Mark this PRIVATE

Mr and Mrs T Knowles
49 Town St
COVENTRY
CV2 3RP

Dr Mr and Mrs Knowles

With ref to your letter concerning the purchase of a luxury apartment in Bath. I am delighted to (here) that you have decided to retire to Bath and as you are both over 50 years of age, all (requirments) for the Avon View apartments (is) fulfilled.

~~I confirm that~~ I would like to confirm the following details. The apartment you have chosen is on the third floor on the front of the building overlooking Bath Abbey. (Features') include a private dining salon, lounge, library, gymnasium, sauna, roof garden, two lifts, security and underground garage parking.

In addition to these features, there is also a guest suite available.

I understand you will be visiting Bath this weekend. Our offices are open all day Sat and I look forward to meeting you again. We can then proceed with the next phase of the purchase.

Yrs sincerely

John Edwards
Sales Negotiator

WP T

Memo

From John Edwards

To Amanda Longman

Ref JE/398

I ref to our recent staff meeting concerning the sale of Avon View apartments in Bath I have now prepared a report on this and a copy is attached for your info.

We need to launch a fresh advertising campaigns to ensure that all these apartments are sold by the end of the yr. Can you please make this a priority? Traditionaly properties sell well during March and April but so far this year this has not been the case.

You will need to emphasise the ~~attractions~~ beauty of the city and all the amenities that are to hand for the over 50s'. As these apartments are aimed at the retirement market, use security as a selling aid. Stress the fact that there is a central system controlling access to the building.

Exam Practice 4 Document 3

WP **T**

Typist/operator: the extra section for this document can be found on page 13.

AMENITIES IN BATH (single line spacing except where indicated)

The following amenities should be used in any future advertising campaign.

Bath is one of the most ~~interesting~~ ~~fascinating~~ cities in the country. It is also one of the easiest to explore. It has a compact centre of broad main streets linked by quaint, narow and traffic-free lanes. Elegant cresents and terraces of pale gold stone greet the eye around every corner. // Although the city is surrounded by hills the walking is relatively flat in the city itself. Ideal for those lazy days of retirement. (Emphasise this paragraph)

<u>Views</u>

Step out of A — V — apartments
~~Walk out of your apartment~~ and you has a wide choice of walks. You can walk along the River Avon and see the famous Pulteney Bridge which is lined with shop on both sides.

<u>Walks</u>

You have a wonderful view of the weir – lean over the parapet and watch the activity below. Pleasure boats filling up, swimmers risking their lives near the weir and canoeists bobbing about everywhere.

<u>Flowers</u>

Orange Grove is imm on your doorstep. The trees and flowers (in spring and summer) are a picture to behold. Bath has won the 'Britain in Bloom' contest so many times that nowadays it is only alowed to enter every other year.

Alongside Orange Grove you have Parade Gardens where you can sit and ~~watch the boats on the river at the same time as~~ listen to a band concert being played from the band stand.

History

these paragraphs only in double linespacing

Some apartments on the front of the building have a magnificent view of Bath Abbey. The 15th century abbey is in the very heart of the city and when floodlit at night is a spectacular sight. the interior is very light and is famous for its soaring traceries of fan-vaulting.

If you are interested in history, Bath has many museums for you to visit. These include the Carriage Museum, the Museum of Costume and the Museum of Bookbinding. to name just a few.

The Assembly Rooms are not far away whilst the Guildhall is next door to the apartments. The Guildhall has an 18th century banqueting room complete with many beautiful chandeliers. Part of the Guildhall complex houses a small market where you can just browse or buy anything from food to antiques.

typist/operator: insert extra paragraph here

General

There is an excellent theatre, sports centre with swimming pool and many restaurants close at hand. Bath is also well-known for its fine shops.

It is nec for me to see your rough draft of teh advertising by (give date for last Friday of next month).

Word Processing

The Stage II Word Processing Part 2 examination offered by RSA Examinations Board tests your ability to produce a variety of documents from handwritten and typewritten drafts as well as recalled text.

You will be asked to type four documents in one and three quarter hours. These are

- an article/report
- a notice for display
- a table
- a standard document which includes stored phrases from a phrase file.

In order to pass the examination you must complete the paper within the time given and incur no more than 11 faults. If you incur only 4 faults or less, you will be awarded a distinction.

Three of the tasks in this examination include text that has previously been keyed in by your tutor including saved phrases. The examination requires you to recall the previously saved text and make amendments as instructed. You will be directed to the appropriate file containing the saved text. When inserting phrases, make sure your cursor is placed exactly where you want the phrase to appear. Do not forget to leave a space before the phrase is inserted and make sure you insert the correct phrase. You will be instructed to insert two out of three phrases. When you have made the required amendments, do not forget to save each piece of work with a different file name.

The text and phrases which need to be keyed in for the purpose of the word processing mock examination papers in this book can be found on pages 14–21.

The tasks will contain corrections and amendments for you to make. You will also be asked to move text to different locations in a document and copy text. When moving a paragraph of text, make sure you place the cursor in the correct position and when copying text, make sure the item appears at least twice.

One or more of the above documents will contain lists of information which require sorting into alphabetical and numerical/chronological order. When sorting the information, make sure each item is included.

When instructed, you must ensure that you have printed a header on each page. If you are asked to change a word or phrase, make sure you change each instance.

When working on the multi-page document, ensure you make all the changes regarding line spacing, line length and justification before you start. Ensure continuation sheets are numbered.

Ensure the correct stationery is used for the standard document. Letters must be produced on letterheads and memos on pre-printed forms. Remember to date letters and memos with the date of the examination. The letterheads and printed memo forms for use with the word processing mock examination papers can be found at the back of the book.

Check that you have printed all the tasks before handing in your examination work. If you are asked to take extra copies, make sure you print the required number and indicate the routing on your extra copies.

One problem candidates face is running out of time in the examination. Not only must you complete the examination paper but you should also have enough time left to check your work carefully. When you are working through the mock examination papers in this section, you may like to make a note of the time each document has taken. As a guide you should aim to complete the tasks within the following time scale.

- Article/report – 20 minutes.
- Notice for display – 20 minutes.
- Table – 30 minutes.
- Standard document – 20 minutes.

This will allow you a total of 15 minutes to read the instructions before you type and to check through your work on completion.

Exam Practice 1 Document 1

WP

Recall this document saved as DECOR1. Amend as shown. Use a justified right margin, and double line-spacing, (except where indicated). Adjust line length to either (a) 12.5 cm or (b) 50 characters. If proportional spacing is used adjust line length to (a). Save as DECOR6 and print one copy.

HOME DECORATION

If you are looking to brighten up your house why not try some different paint effects. These are quick, easy and inexpensive but can make a great difference to your home. You do not have to be a talented artist as these effects are easy to do.

(A)

Colourwashing - This has a subtle effect which adds tone and colour. It is good for covering uneven plasterwork. ~~This may be useful if you live in an old property.~~

When this coat has dried, you will be able to see if there are any areas that are uneven. Now apply a second coat. Try to make the strokes cross the first coat strokes at right angles.

Apply two base coats of emulsion paint with a roller. Allow to dry thoroughly. When dry, apply a coat of colourwash using criss cross strokes. Vary the angle of the strokes to show the base coat underneath.

Stencilling - This is simple to do but very effective. Stencil kits containing paints, brushes and stencils are available at art shops and DIY stores. If you are more adventurous you can easily make your own designs using strong card or acetate. (This paragraph only in single line-spacing)

Stippling - To achieve this effect you paint a layer of glaze over your base colour. Then using a stipple brush, you break up the colour into a series of dots which when dry gives a texture rather like airbrushing. Anyone can do this and the results look very professional.

Apply two coats of base colour using eggshell paint. When this has dried you can apply the glaze in strips. Let this dry a little. Now using a stipple brush dipped in colour, stab the wall at right angles so that the colour breaks up into the glaze. If you are using this effect in a kitchen or bathroom, you may need to apply a coat of clear varnish.

When this has dried, follow these steps again using a toning colour. (Move this paragraph to point marked (A))

Sponging - This gives a mottled effect and can look very attractive. You will need a small sea sponge to achieve this effect.

After applying ~~two~~ three coats of base colour, allow to dry thoroughly. Pour a little paint in (✓) a tray and dab the sponge in. Squeeze the sponge gently to remove excess paint. Now, dab the wall with the sponge in a random direction. Change the direction of the sponge occasionally to get a speckled effect.

(A)

There are many good books for sale which give full details of these techniques. Your local DIY store may also offer help and advice.

Copy this to point marked (B)

There are also a number of courses and workshops available. Find out if your local college has any courses on offer.

Inset this 2.5cm from both margins

Insert GOOD IDEAS! as a header to appear on every page.

Exam Practice 1 Document 2

WP

Recall the document stored as DECOR2
Amend as shown. Use either a justified or ragged right margin.
Save as DECOR7 and print one copy.

The Art School ← Centre this heading

Home Decoration Courses ← Emphasise this heading

If you are tired of your decorations but cannot afford the services of a professional decorator, why not try do-it-yourself? It is much easier than you think. By applying some different paint effects you can achieve ~~some~~ very professional results.

The Art School offers one-day courses on various paint techniques. The following will be held over the next three months.

Colourwashing
Stippling
Marbling
Rag rolling
Stencilling
Sponging

← Sort into exact alphabetical order.

The course fees include refreshments and a buffet lunch. Please bring some protective clothing.

Leave a 51 mm gap here.

For further information and/or an enrolment form, please contact:

Jennifer MacDonald
The Art School
Hanley Way
GLASGOW
G72 8HN
Telephone 01783 165238.

Change course to workshop throughout this document

Exam Practice 1 Document 3

WP

(Key in the following table. Store as DEC008 and print one copy.)

To All Staff

(Do not rule table)

Home Decoration Workshops

Please note that the following workshops have been arranged. The course leaders should check with the Admissions Secretary a week before the workshop that enough students have enrolled. Please ensure that you have plenty of materials ordered in advance.

The refreshments will be served in the Green Room. Lunch will be at 12.30 pm.

Course	Date	Time	Course Leader
June Workshops			
Stippling	8 June	9am - 4pm	Shirley Davies
Colourwashing	21 June	10am - 3pm	Alyssa Marks
Sponging	3 June	9.30am - 4pm	Frank Powell
Stencilling	6 June	11am - 4pm	Tracey Hull
August Workshops			
Stippling	12 August	9.30am - 3.30pm	Chris Middleton
Colourwashing	19 August	10am - 3.45pm	John Somerset
Marbling	2 August	11am - 5pm	Eddie Fryer
Rag rolling	11 August	10am - 3pm	Moira Bailey
July Workshops			
Marbling	4 July	9am - 4pm	Chris Middleton
Rag rolling	25 July	10am - 3pm	Sam McFee
Stencilling	19 July	9.30am - 3pm	Peter Hamilton
Sponging	3 July	10.15am - 4pm	Fiona Harper

(Type the July section before August.)

(Sort each section by ascending date order – ensure all corresponding details are moved.)

(Move the Course Leader column to become the second col.)

Exam Practice 1 Document 4

WP

Please key in the following document. Insert the phrases where shown. Save as DECOR9 and print one copy using headed notepaper.

Our ref PW/MW/HDC

Top + 2 please. One copy for Frank Powell and one for file. Indicate routing.

Mrs Penny Whitmarsh
7 King's Road
GLASGOW
G27 2NK

Dear Mrs Whitmarsh

Thank you for your completed enrolment form and cheque. I confirm you have been allocated a place on the (Insert Phrase stored as DECOR4.) workshop on 3 June. A copy of this letter will be sent to Frank Powell, who is the course leader.

The workshop will take place at The Art Schools main building in Hanley Way. Please come to (Insert Phrase Stored as DECOR3) which is on the second floor. A lift is available for disabled students.

Refreshments are included in the workshop fee. These include a buffet lunch and coffee. If you require a special diet, please let us know at least 2 days in advance. // All materials are also included in the fee. However you will need to bring some protective clothing. An opportunity to purchase the special equipment required will be available at the end of the day. This equipment includes paint brushes, sponges, rollers, etc.

We look forward to meeting you and hope you enjoy your day.

Yrs sncly

Marsha Wilmot
Admissions Secretary

Exam Practice 2 Document 1

WP

Recall this document stored under CARAVAN1. Amend as shown. Change to double linespacing (except where indicated) and use a justified right margin. Adjust line length to either (a) 12.5 cm or (b) 50 characters. If proportional spacing is used, please adjust line length to (a). Save as CARAVAN6 and print one copy.

emphasise this heading

Touring Caravan Holidays

(A)

Firstly check your caravan tyre pressures including the spare, and wheel-nut tightness. Turn off the gas cylinder and make sure it is strapped upright.

Move this section to point marked (A)

Before you start your holiday you must ensure your van has been serviced regularly so that it is safe in all respects when touring on the road and when on site. As an extra to the normal service, have the body checked for signs of damp. It is a good idea to have this done early in the year before your first trip.

Empty all ~~liquid containers~~ water tanks and carry any water required for your journey in a small container in the car. Secure any loose items in the van, close windows and rooflights. Fasten travel catch on cupboards and refrigerator.

Inset this paragraph 51 mm (2") from left margin

Many people now wear gloves to protect their hands when doing these outdoor chores.

You can now hitch your caravan on to your towing vehicle. ~~Wind the jockey wheel down.~~ Clamp the jockey wheel securely in place and fit stabiliser if used. Connect wiring cables and check all lights and indicators are working. Fit extension wing mirrors for a better view when towing. Walk round the caravan for a final check.

this section only in single linespacing

When you have been towing for about 20 minutes stop and walk round the van again. Check that all the windows are still fastened and that everything looks secure inside.

If you are going to use a trailer tent or an awning as a cooking area it is wise to have a large bucket of water handy when sited. This is in addition to the fire extinguisher and fire blanket. ~~It is always wise to be prepared.~~

~~There are a number of safety devices you can carry~~ For safety reasons we recommend you carry a 1 kg dry powder extinguisher. A fire blanket is advisable for the kitchen area and also a smoke detector.

Copy this section to point marked ⊕

You will need to check the noseweight of the caravan.
~~The noseweight of the caravan will have to be checked.~~ The recommended figure will be in your handbook. Ensure your handbrake is fully on and then raise corner steadies and stow winding handle and step.
Lock the door.

On arrival at your site check in first with the owner or warden. Be sure to follow instructions given by them for siting your caravan. In order to make sure your refrigerator operates properly level the caravan to within 3 degrees.// After you are safely settled on a pitch fit the hitchlock and wheel clamp to secure your caravan. You now deserve that welcome cup of tea!

insert SCENIC SITES to appear as a header on every page

Change van to caravan throughout this document

3

Exam Practice 2 Document 2

WP

Recall this document stored under CARAVAN 2. Amend as shown. Save as CARAVAN 7 and print one copy.

CARAVAN INSURANCE COVER (centre)

We can arrange insurance cover for your caravan, your car or motor caravan. Our premiums are very favourable and we can provide the insurance you personally need.

If you travel abroad in Europe we can provide free foreign travel cover provided your journey does not exceed 31 days. For motor caravan drivers up to 3 months' cover is provided. Special arrangements can be made for longer periods.

Leave at least 25mm (2.5cm) here

Our motor caravan foreign travel covers the following.

Awnings
Aerials
Baggage
Batteries
Heaters
Radios
Cassette players
Toilet tents
Water carriers
Television

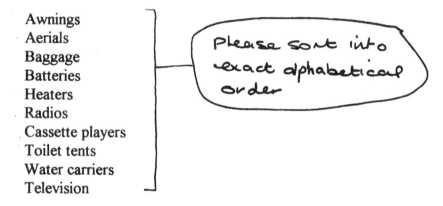

Please sort into exact alphabetical order

Our most popular insurance choice includes comprehensive cover on or off the road. It's a new for old cover with caravan age restriction of up to 5 years old. Your caravan contents are also covered. You can have automatic cover for use of your caravan by family and friends.

We also have a special travel service insurance especially for caravaners. This gives motoring, medical, baggage and personal cover as a package deal.

Our claims service is fast and fair.

Exam Practice 2 Document 3

WP

Key in the following table, save as CARAVAN 8 and print one copy.

CARAVAN HOLIDAY SITES

Please move the COUNTY section to become the first section before NAME OF SITE

DO NOT RULE

Please move the Wales section to above the Scotland section

BRITISH SITES		NUMBER OF PITCHES	AREA IN ACRES
NAME OF SITE	COUNTY OR REGION		
England			
Four Ways	Cornwall	70	4
High Park	Cumbria	200	20
Flower Corner	Devon	120	7
Five Arches	Somerset	135	9
Cross Hill	Dorset	150	25
The Grove	Essex	180	12
Wood Park	Hampshire	185	15
South Oak	Kent	190	17
Scotland			
Blair Way	Central	90	8
Mountain Way	Fife	110	8
Golden Bank	Grampian	55	4
The Moor	Highland	120	8
Riverbank View	Highland	150	23
The Gardens	Lothian	155	15
Wales			
Lady Anne	Clwyd	35	2
Shaw Country	Dyfed	50	4
Sunshine Way	Gwent	55	5
Low Park	Gwent	60	5
Owl Tree	Powys	30	3
The Lake	Dyfed	70	4
Forest Walk	Powys	90	8

Site opening times, facilities and prices vary. Many sites are now open all year. There is usually a dog walk on site or nearby and dogs must be on a lead at all times.

Please sort NUMBER OF PITCHES into exact numerical order within each section. Ensure corresponding details are also rearranged.

Exam Practice 2 Document 4

WP

Please key in the following document and insert the phrases indicated. Save as CARAVAN 9 and print, using headed paper.

Our ref DA/WD

Mr and Mrs A Stone
153 Princess Street
WAKEFIELD
West Yorkshire
WF1 6PQ

Dear Mr and Mrs Stone

WARDENS AT GOLDEN HILL SITE

Check this from Document 3 and amend if necessary

Thank you both for attending our training day last week. I am pleased to offer you the post of wardens at the above site for the coming season.

The site is situated in a most beautiful part of Scotland. Would you please visit it within the next week and let me have your decision as to whether you will accept the post.

Insert Phrase 3 stored as CARAVAN 5.

Throughout March you will have time to get the site ready after the winter for visitors. Hedges will need trimming and grass cut if dry enough. You will know from past experience the type of jobs that are needed to be done.

Likewise the month of October is used to close the site down for the winter months. There is always a lot of work to be done after a busy summer season.

The site will open this year with more handstanding pitches and the play area has been extended.

Insert Phrase 2 stored as CARAVAN 4.

Yours sincerely

David Armstrong
Personnel Officer

Top and 2 copies please. One file copy and one for Sites Manager. Indicate routing.

Exam Practice 3 Document 1

WP

Recall this document saved as HOMES1. Amend as shown. Use a justified right hand margin, and double line-spacing (except where indicated). Adjust line length to either (a) 12.5cm or (b) 50 characters. If proportional spacing is used, please adjust line length to (a). Save as HOMES6 and print one copy.

Cornwall's Finest Holiday Homes

This leaflet aims to tell you about our booking agency and to give you information on how to turn your holiday home into a successful business.

We are a long-established booking agency concentrating on homes in Cornwall. Each year we produce a full-colour brochure featuring over 350 homes to let. [Copy this paragraph to point marked (A).]

Our experience in this business means that we can give an expert opinion as to the potential of your holiday property. We can also advise you on the amount of rent you can realistically expect to receive.

The full-colour brochure features a photograph of every property together with professionally written details, making it interesting and easy to read. We receive over 45,000 enquiries each year.

By choosing us as your booking agent you can be assured you will receive a first-class service. Our competent staff deal with all the details on your behalf. They provide a friendly and efficient service. Our offices are open from 9.30 am to 6.30 pm seven days a week. This means you will never miss an opportunity for letting your home.

(A)

The Tourist Board has an inspection service that grades holiday properties on a scale of 1 to 5. This is assessed on a yearly basis and offers peace of mind to our customers. The assessment gives helpful feedback on making the most of your property. We do not accept properties that have a grading of less than 4. [This paragraph only in single line-spacing]

We advise our property owners to take out cancellation insurance. This can be arranged through our offices. This means that should a holiday be cancelled because of accident or ill-health, etc, you will receive 85% of the usual price. You will also require Public Liability insurance for your property. // It is advised that you insure your home and contents against accidental damage by customers. Our agency has arranged a special deal with a local insurance company. It can offer you very reasonable rates for this service. ~~Please let us know if you would like further details~~.

You will probably wish to take some weeks for your friends and family. We ask you to limit this to four during the year. A maximum of two can be taken during the peak season. You do not have to let your home for the entire year. The minimum number of weeks is 24. A short break offer for the winter months is very popular with our customers. You may wish to consider this for your property. [Inset this paragraph by 2.5cm from both margins]

They must be able to rely on the property they book to be comfortable and well-equipped.

As we deal with many properties our commission charges are extremely reasonable. A basic rate of 15% plus VAT is payable for each booking. A yearly charge of £75 is also payable for the Tourist Board inspection. If you are registered for VAT you may claim back the VAT payable on commission.

(*)

More this paragraph to point marked (A).

Insert a header Letting your Property to appear on every page.

Change booking to letting throughout this document.

Exam Practice 3 Document 2

WP

Recall this document saved as HOMES2.
Amend as shown using a justified or ragged right-hand margin. Save as HOMES7 and print one copy.

Cornwall's Finest Holiday Homes ← (Emphasise this heading.)

Inspection and Grading

Holidaymakers expect high standards of quality and comfort when they book a property. Without a grading system, booking a property can be very hit or miss. Cornwall's Finest Holiday Homes will only accept properties that have undergone an inspection by the local tourist board. A grading of four or above must be attained.

In order for a property to obtain a high grade, it must be in excellent condition. The furniture and fittings must be of a high standard and free from wear and tear. The property must be comfortable and clean. Cleaning of the property between lettings must be undertaken. // Kitchens and bathrooms should be easy to clean and in good condition. Extra marks will be awarded for provision of the following items:

Dishwasher
Tumble dryer
Automatic washing machine
Freezer
Microwave oven

(Sort into exact alphabetical order + Centre)

[Leave a gap of at least 51 mm here.]

After the property has been inspected a full and detailed report will be written. This feedback is extremely useful in helping owners upgrade their homes.

Exam Practice 3 Document 3

WP

(Key in the following table, save as HOMES8 and print one copy.)

Brochure Amendments

The following properties are now booked for the entire season. Please ensure the computer is updated. A letter will have to be sent to each of the owners informing them of this.

These properties are always very popular. We should consider featuring them on a separate page of the next brochure. (Do not rule table)

Address	Rental per Week £	Code	Owner
Penzance			
1 The Slipway	380	PS1	Margaret Ashton
8 Castle Gardens	270	PS8	Colin Hynes
23 Heron Court	320	PS2	Stanley Garland
17 Willow Close	255	PS6	Eileen Jeffries
12 Selwood Drive	295	PS13	Ashley Griffin
Portreath			
Rose Cottage	365	PR12	Alice Scullin
32 Harbour View	295	PR5	Matthew Palmer
Beach Cottage	420	PR38	Annabelle Rich
29 Eden Place	235	PR27	William Leeds
6 Seaview Way	340	PR32	Peter Marks
Truro			
82 High Street	255	TR28	Betty George
7 Woodlands Road	360	TR17	Jonathan Bridges
11 Chestnut Street	275	TR63	Karen Freeman
41 Mayfield Lane	280	TR6	Janice Wilson
28 Park Street	320	TR62	Neil Simmons

(Please sort each section into ascending order of rental per week.)

(Please type the Truro section before Portreath)

(Move the owner column to become the second column.)

Exam Practice 3 Document 4

WP

Please key in the following document. Insert phrases where shown. Save as HOMES9 and print one copy.

Our ref SVH/VJ/139

Mrs Penny Whitmarsh
22 Westgate Street
HAYTON
Cumbria
CU27 3IN

Dear Mrs Whitmarsh

SEAVIEW HOUSE, ST IVES

The Tourist Board inspection report on your above property has now been received at our offices. A copy for your attention will be posted shortly. We are pleased to advise you that Seaview House has been awarded a (Insert Phrase 3 stored as HOMES5 here).

In view of this, we feel that a reasonable rent would be (Insert Phrase 2 stored as HOMES4 here). This rental will be reviewed at the end of the season. It may be that we can increase this by £50 per week for next season. // If you decide to place your property with our agency we will immediately produce a sheet to be included with our brochure. I am confident we can arrange many lettings for your holiday home this season.

I will need to have copies of insurance certificates for the property. A copy of this letter will be sent to Michael Ruskin, our insurance broker. He will contact you shortly.

If you require any further information please do not hesitate to contact me.

Yours sincerely

Colin Fraser
Manager

Top + 2 please.
One copy for Michael Ruskin and one for file.
Indicate routing.

3

Exam Practice 4 Document 1

WP

Recall the document stored under GARDEN1. Amend as shown. Use double linespacing (except where indicated). Adjust line length to either (a) 12.5cm or (b) 50 characters. If proportional spacing is used please adjust line length to (a). Use a justified right margin. Save as GARDEN6 and print one copy.

Insert WILDLIFE FACT SHEET to appear as a header on every page

The song thrush has a fine voice and sings for much of the year.

A Garden For Wildlife (emphasise)

No matter how small your garden, [with careful planning] it can be a paradise for birds and other wildlife. A small pond is imperative as it makes a home for frogs and insects. It is also a place for birds to drink and bathe.

(A)

Plant a few shrubs that have berries as these make natural food for birds. They also give winter food for all kinds of small creatures.

[Inset 38mm from left margin] Although a Bhuddleia shrub can grow quite tall its blooms attract many different butterflies.

Blackbirds and thrushes find a lawn a perfect feeding ground. [The robin is a frequent visitor to almost all gardens.] ~~No matter how small your garden is birds will be frequent visitors~~. You cannot fail to see him with his bright orange-red face and breast.

(*)

[Move to point marked (A)] Build the pond with gently sloping sides. Have a stone wall close by for shelter for the frogs and toads.

Keep those precious autumn leaves and pile them under shrubs and hedges. Fill hedgehog boxes with them and put some in bin liners to rot down for use next year. // You are likely to find a wren poking among ground litter and picking food from the leaves. The wren has a tiny body but a loud voice, listen for its fast and shrill song. ~~You will be surprised how much noise it can make~~.

Copy to point marked (*)

Listen for spring being heralded at both dawn and dusk by the blackbird's song.

These birds are perhaps our commonest of garden birds and nest in bushes.

This section only in single linespacing

From September think about bird ~~food holders~~ ~~feeding~~ devices. Small birds have to eat all day to survive the cold winter nights. The blue tit has very acrobatic feeding habits. Watch him feeding on a nut holder.

If you are keen on gardens and wildlife and would like to visit our organic gardens, send for our free booklet listing these. ~~Our gardens are at their best in the summer~~. The best time to visit is June and July.

Put your bird table and feeders ~~near to plants that climb~~ close to the cover of a climbing plant or a shrub to give the birds shelter. Although you may not fancy a bath outside at this time of year, it is important for birds to have one. They bathe to keep their feathers in good condition. Replace frozen water in a bird bath each morning or float a ball in your pond to keep a small patch ice-free.

hanging upside-down

Please change pond to pool throughout the document

3

Exam Practice 4 Document 2

WP

Recall this document stored under GARDEN 2. Amend as shown. Save as GARDEN 4 and print one copy.

A POOL IN YOUR GARDEN ← centre

Water can be delightful in a garden. Its sight and sound are both relaxing and refreshing. The shape and size of a pool will depend on the site chosen for it. A generous rectangular, circular or oval shape is the most effective. If you have a large garden a more irregular shape to form part of the natural landscape would be more in character.

↕ Leave at least 51mm (5.1cm) here

We will be running a series of courses on how to design and construct a pool. Instruction will be given on how to measure up and landscape the site, suitable materials and methods of construction.

The design course dates are as follows.

10 September 1997
6 September 1997
8 October 1997 ← Sort into exact date order
13 September 1997
18 October 1997
27 September 1997

The design course will begin with coffee and registration at 10.30 am. Bring your own packed lunch, and drinks will be provided. You will need a notebook, a pad of drawing paper, recommended size A3, and suitable drawing instruments and pencils. The day will close with tea and biscuits at 4pm.

WP

Key in the following table, save as GARDEN 8 and print one copy.

WILDLIFE GARDEN COURSES

DO NOT RULE

Please move the ROOM NUMBER section to become the last section after TYPE OF COURSE

Please move the 6 September section to above 22 October section

STUDENT REGISTRATION DETAILS		ROOM NUMBER	TYPE OF COURSE
NAME	NUMBER		
22 October – 8 November (Plants)			
ALLEN P	001	3	Trees
ELLISON A	009	3	Trees
HUNT D	024	5	Flowers
KNIGHT H	032	5	Flowers
PARSONS D	015	1	Shrubs
JONES W	017	1	Shrubs
6 September – 18 October (Pools)			
BARNES D	012	4	Design
DAY A	019	7	Construction
SCOTT L	037	4	Design
CARTER G	006	8	Planting
SMEDLEY C	004	7	Construction
TURNER F	030	4	Design
WALKER A	010	8	Planting
12 November – 29 November (Hard Features)			
McDONALD S	002	2	Paving
STENNER R	014	9	Building
RICHARDS M	020	6	Fencing
STRINGER A	035	9	Building
WILLIAMS S	036	2	Paving
YOUNG K	033	6	Fencing

All the above courses are now full and a waiting list is being kept. They have all paid the minimum fee of £25 for the day.

Please sort student surname into exact alphabetical order within each section. Ensure corresponding details are also rearranged.

Exam Practice 4 Document 4

WP

Please key in the following document and insert the phrases as indicated. Save as GARDEN 9 and print.

MEMORANDUM

From Caroline Brook

To All Course leaders

Ref CB|WGC

You will see from the attached list that all places are now fully booked for the autumn series. We have compiled a waiting list and this will be used in strict order of registration should a place become available.

Check number from Document 3 and amend if necessary

The course on pool construction will take place partly in room 19 and partly outside in the workshop area. Students have been asked to wear suitable clothes and footwear.

insert Phrase 3 stored as GARDEN 5

All the courses on hard features in the garden will have the necessary theory in the rooms allocated. The rest of the time will be spent outside doing practical work.

insert Phrase 2 stored as GARDEN 4

Courses will start promptly at 10.45 am and a lunch break will be taken from 1pm to 1.45pm in the canteen area where drinks will be provided. Tea and biscuits will end the day at 4pm and will again be served in the canteen area.

Please let me have a copy of the contents of your course for our records.

Top + 2 please. One for Site Administrator and one for our files. Indicate Routing.

Typewriting

The Stage II Typewriting Part 2 examination offered by RSA Examinations Board tests your ability to produce a variety of business documents from handwritten and typewritten drafts.

You will be asked to type four documents in one and three quarter hours. These are

- a notice for display
- an article
- a ruled table with subdivisions and multi-line headings
- a pre-printed form to be completed from given information (and an envelope or label).

In order to pass the examination you must complete the paper within the time given and incur no more than 10 faults. If you incur only 4 faults or less, you will be awarded a distinction.

Before you start typing, read through the document which requires a word or words to be changed throughout and pencil the word or words on the exam paper. You will not miss them or forget them by doing this.

You will be asked to leave a vertical space of at least the measurement given. Measure the space before typing the rest of the paper. Any error in spacing can then be put right.

You will be asked to sort lists of information into date or numerical order. Always ensure you have sorted the items into exact order before continuing to type.

Ensure you have left enough spaces after each column in the tabulation – check you have counted using the longest line. Take care you do not omit a footnote sign or explanation. Rule carefully with a black pen which matches the type print.

Remember to date the form with the date of the examination and take care to type just above the dotted lines. Ensure all information asked for is there. DO NOT SIGN THE FORM. Ensure you type the label/envelope to the correct name and address. Take two extra copies of the form and indicate routing. The pre-printed forms which must be completed in the mock examination typewriting papers contained in this book can be found on pages 88–91.

One problem candidates face is running out of time in the examination. Not only must you complete the examination paper but you should also have enough time left to check your work carefully. When you are working through the mock examination papers in this section, you may like to make a note of the time each document has taken. As a guide you should aim to complete the tasks within the following time scale.

- Notice for display – 15 minutes.
- Article – 30 minutes.
- Ruled table – 35 minutes.
- Form – 15 minutes.

This will allow you a total of 10 minutes to read the instructions before you type and to check through your work on completion.

Exam Practice 1 Document 1

T

RAIL STEAM TOURS ← centre this heading

Following the success of our last steam tours we are pleased to give you details of a new tour we are adding to our list this year.

This will take place through the West Country from Taunton to Minehead. You will travel through country stations viewing thatched cottages along the way. At Watchet your route is alongside the harbour, and you will see Dunster Castle before arriving at Minehead station on the sea front.

The tours will take place on the following dates.

1 June
4 June
18 June
15 June
6 July
13 July ← Sort into exact date order
20 July
9 July
3 August
6 August
13 August
10 August

Be sure to visit our railway exhibition whilst in Minehead. ← emphasise this sentence

Exam Practice 1 Document 2

T

MINEHEAD RAILWAY EXHIBITION

Change excursion to tour throughout this document

The exhibition is open on all excursion dates from 10am to 5pm. It is run by volunteer stewards who will be very happy to answer any questions you may have.

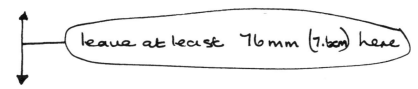

leave at least 76mm (7.6cm) here

A snack bar will be open serving a selection of drinks and light meals. There will also be a number of trade stands selling models, books, calendars, art prints and video tapes. Choose from the following list a video tape of your favourite railways to take home and remember your day out.

modify layout so that list appears as two columns

Please sort into exact alphabetical order

Glasgow tramcar
Diesel locos
Electric trains
Great Western
Lost railways
North Devon line
Light rail
Past and present
Rails through the sand
Rolling stock
Royal Scot 2
Signalling
Stations
Rocket to Eurostar
Steam locos

4

To go with this excursion, take advantage of our special offer video tape of the Taunton to Minehead line. This offer is only available to excursion ticket holders.

The following details are given as a guide to the exhibits.

Modify layout so that the following text appears on a separate line below its heading, eg
Minster Junction
This is a . . . . .

Minster Junction This is a single-track branch line which is joined at Minster Junction by another single-track line from Johnson Wharf. The layout is mainly hand built and the rolling stock is kit built.

Great Bar Goods This goods yard is set in the Midlands during the changeover from steam to diesel. The layout is constructed on a single board complete with track and points.

Eastmoor This is a small layout built to be usable in a modern house. The locos are mainly diesels from the 1950s through to the present day.

Edwards Green Setting the scene for this layout, summer is long gone and the harvest is gathered in. One captures the feeling of a small Devon station serving a village and farming community.

Throughout the day there will be various demonstrations of model and kit making skills.

Exam Practice 1 Document 3

T

(Rule as shown)

MODEL RAILWAYS SALE

Visit our stands at the exhibition in Minehead and browse through our sale stock. We are sure you will find a bargain.

Description of models		Class and price		Stand Information
Code Number	Type	Name	£	
A142 A143 A144 A145 A146 A147	Steam Diesel Steam Electric Diesel Steam	Branchline Freight Pullman Intercity Night Mail Coronation*	50.50 52.50 96.50 70.80 87.15 80.50	On stand numbers 7–9 you will find a variety of train sets all of which include locos, rolling stock, power unit and a circle of track. All items are boxed as a set.
B237 B238 B239 B240 B241 B242	Steam Steam Diesel Diesel Electric Electric	Mallard Saint Deltic Western Southern Express	53.70 45.50 33.50 34.50 30.50 34.35	A wide range of locos is displayed on stands 5 and 6. Most models are on sale in the colours of the new train companies.
C362 C363 C364 C365 C366 C367	Goods Goods Goods Coach Coach Coach	Hopper Tank Grain Dining Intercity Pullman	5.95 4.80 6.50 10.20 12.20 12.50	For a full range of rolling stock visit stands 1 and 2. Coaches are available in most train company colours. Goods wagons are priced singly but a discount will be given for bulk orders.

* This model is only available while stocks last.

Exam Practice 1 Document 4

T

Please complete the Railway Exhibition form and type an envelope or label to Rail Steam Tours, Wellington Road, TAUNTON, Somerset, TA1 4XJ. Take two extra copies (on plain paper or photocopied) one for Booking Clerk and one for file.

Name Mr Andrew Miller

Address 3 Raglans Lane
SWINDON
Wilts SN2 2LP

Amount enclosed £25.00

He would like to purchase a video tape on the Taunton to Minehead Line.

He would also like to have a single ticket for himself.

He would like to depart on the 9.15am on 6 August.

He would like to include the loco repair workshop and museum at Washford and the old town harbour at Watchfull for his short visits.

Check this word from Document 1 and amend if necessary

Exam Practice 2 Document 1

T

BATH TIMES

Our new range of luxury bath accessories will be on sale at the end of May. ← (Check this detail from Document 2 and amend if necessary.)

The Seaside range of toiletries will be in the shops in time for the summer holidays. In bright, stylish packaging with seaside motifs, the range is great fun. The familiar and fresh seaside fragrances will ensure your summer holiday stays with you throughout the year.

The range includes:

Bath foam SEA421
Shower gel SEA439
Bath oil SEA422
Soap SEA464
Shampoo SEA471
Talcum powder SEA465
Bath crystals SEA463
Conditioner SEA420
Hand and body lotion SEA423

(Sort into exact code order and modify layout so that the code number appears first.)

The Seaside collection costs from £1 for a luxury soap to £25 for a gift hamper full of goodies.

The Bath Times range is available from department stores or by mail order.

(Centre this paragraph)

4

Exam Practice 2 Document 2

T

Bathing Belles ← Centre this heading

The Bathing Belles Company sells high-quality bath accessories and goods. From soaps to bath towels, bathroom cabinets to shower curtains, you can find everything you need for your bathroom in our range.

(Leave a gap of at least 7.5cm (75mm) here)

Each year Bathing Belles produces several new collections of bath products. We are always updating our bath accessories' collections to match the latest in bathroom style.

We manufacture all our own toiletries. This way we can control production and ensure that the ingredients have not been tested on animals. All packaging is environmentally friendly. Where possible, the packaging is made from recycled materials.

Bathing Belles has been manufacturing bath products for over 20 years. It started as a small cottage industry supplying a local gift shop. Over the years it has grown and now supplies all the major department stores throughout the UK. A mail order service is available. A full-colour catalogue is published twice a year.

Our most popular range is the Country Collection which includes:

Bath foam
Moisturiser
Shower gel
Conditioner
Face wash
Bath pearls
Shampoo
Hand cream
Toner
Body lotion
Talcum powder
Soap
Bath oil
Deodorant
Body scrub
Bath crystals

Sort into exact alphabetical order and display in two columns

All these products will be found in the new Spring Catalogue. This also features our latest collection, the Seaside range. It will be available on 24 January.

Included in the catalogue are the following:

Modify the layout so that the heading appears on the same line as the text, eg
Jungle Range – This range ...

Jungle Range

This range has been prepared especially for children. All products are made from the most mild ingredients. It is safe for children of all ages, including babies. The bright, well-designed packaging makes bath time fun. Children will love our exciting new additions to the range including a glitter bath foam and shower gel.

Just for Men

This fresh-smelling range of men's toiletries is very popular and is one of our best-selling collections. Products include aftershave, face wash and deodorant as well as the usual bath and shower items.

Call 01842 61430 for a free copy of our Catalogue or visit your local department store.

Emphasise this sentence

Change Bathing Belles to Bath Times throughout this document.

Exam Practice 2 Document 3

T

Spring Catalogue Publicity Leaflet

The table below forms part of our new leaflet. This will contain colour photographs and an order form. The leaflet will be inserted in various, suitable magazines and newspapers. It is designed to promote the new Spring catalogue.

Product details		Description	Catalogue details	
Item	Content		Price	Code*
Rose Soap Rose bath oil Rose hand cream Rose shampoo Rose conditioner Rose shower gel	100gm 150 ml 150 ml 250 ml 250 ml 175 ml	Country Collection** Fragrances of rose, lavender, carnation and lily of the valley are included in this range. Our best-selling items ever.	1.20 2.50 1.75 2.35 2.50 2.50	RS021 RB013 RHC15 RSH19 RCR35 RSG26
Shower gel Shampoo Conditioner Bath foam Soap	225 ml 250 ml 250 ml 175 ml 240 gm	Seaside Range This fresh new range will remind you of long hot days by the sea. Suitable for all the family.	2.75 2.99 3.20 2.75 3.50	SEA439 SEA471 SEA420 SEA421 SEA464
Zebra shampoo Lion bubble bath Tiger shower gel Hippo bath oil Crocodile soap	150 ml 280 ml 250 ml 230 ml 120 gm	Jungle Range Children of all ages love this fun range of toiletries. The mild ingredients mean the products are suitable for babies.	1.85 2.60 2.30 2.95 1.20	JZS21 JLB23 JTS12 JHB38 JCS28

* When ordering, please ensure you quote the correct code.

** These products are also available in Carnation, Lavender and Lily of the Valley fragrances.

Exam Practice 2 Document 4

T

Please complete the BATH TIMES form. Take two extra copies, one to Mrs Kathy Jones and one for file. Indicate routing.

<u>Name + Address</u>

Mr Simon Wing
2 The Towers
BELFAST
Northern Ireland
BT3 4XY

<u>Phone</u>

Day: 01964 323195
Eve 01964 379882

<u>Order</u>

Zebra Shampoo	1	JZS21	£1·85
Lion Bubble Bath	1	JLB23	£2·60
Crocodile Soap	1	JCS28	£1·20

<u>Payment</u>

Cheque

<u>Mailing List</u>

Yes

<u>Date</u>

Today's

Please type an envelope/label to

Mrs Kathy Jones
22 Highland Grove
EDINBURGH
EH5 6XX

Exam Practice 3 Document 1

T

YOUR SKIN AND YOUR TAN ← (centre this heading)

When preparing for your holiday tan ensure you know about your skin type. We all like to get a healthy looking suntan but we forget the damage the sun can do to our skin.

If you have dark skin and dark hair your skin will usually tan easily but you still need protection from a sunscreen lotion or cream.

Choose from the following protections one to suit your own skin type.

12 Fair skin
14 Sunblock for face
13 Outdoor sports
15 In open cars
16 Maximum exposure
19 Dark skin
17 Normal skin
25 Total cover
23 Around eyes

(Sort into exact numerical order)

→ Apply a body lotion daily as part of your after sun care.

(Emphasise this sentence)

4

Exam Practice 3 Document 2

T

CARING FOR YOUR HAIR

change cleanse to rinse throughout this document

Your hair is the frame for your face. To enhance your natural features your hair cut, style and condition are all very important. A shining head of hair makes you both look and feel good. You may have thick or fine hair, curly or straight, oily or dry, but whatever it is you must give it the right care it needs daily.

leave at least 51mm (5.1cm) here

When caring for your hair, ensure you observe the following.

modify layout so that list appears as one column

Sort into exact alphabetical order

Brush daily
Avoid rubbing when wet
Choose a good brush
Condition often
Comb frequently
Cut and style

Heated rollers
Little use of dryers
Shampoo gently
Thoroughly cleanse
Wear gloves when colouring
Wash brush and comb often

Modify layout so that the following text appears on a separate line below its heading, eg
HAIR CARE ROUTINE

To keep your hair .....

HAIR CARE ROUTINE To keep your hair clean you should wash it at least once a week. Wet hair with warm water and massage the shampoo gently into the hair and scalp. Experiment with different ones to discover the one that suits you best. Always cleanse well and then repeat if your hair is very dirty or greasy.

CONDITION AND DRY Massage the conditioner from the roots to the ends of the hair. Leave on as directed and then cleanse the hair thoroughly. Brush your hair into style and leave to dry naturally or blow dry. Do not concentrate the heat in one place and hold the dryer at least 15cm away from your hair.

STYLING Your hairstyle can affect the shape of your face. It can create a new image for you and give you more confidence. Whatever style you choose it should be easy to look after and one you feel happy with. Visit your hairdresser once every six weeks to keep it in shape.

HAIR COLOUR Most of us colour our hair at some time in our lives. The most natural colour for hair is only one or two shades darker or lighter than your own. Never dye your eyebrows and eyelashes.

Too much sun can damage your hair. Always wear a sun hat when out in the hot sun.

4

Exam Practice 3 Document 3

T

SUMMER HOLIDAY SPECIAL

Take a break from your normal routine and give your skin and hair a fresh new feeling for the holiday season.

At Home and on Holiday		Product Cost*		General Comments
Reference	Item	Code Number	£	
SR302	Sun cap	5136	4.50	Make sure you and your family are protected with sun creams and lotions suitable for the country you are visiting.
SR303	Sunglasses	5137	10.50	
SR304	Sun cream	5138	7.00	
SR305	Sun lotion	5139	5.35	
Check this word from Document 2 and amend if necessary				
BT401	Creme bath	7221	3.50	For a relaxing bath ensure the water temperature is comfortably warm. A tepid bath helps you to unwind at the end of the day.
BT402	Shower creme	7222	3.50	
BT403	Beauty soap	7223	2.45	
BT404	Silk talc	7224	2.50	
BT405	Bath mit	7225	4.45	
HP504	Shampoo	9543	3.00	Use a conditioner to smooth the outer surface of the hair which is roughened by washing. Mist your hair with hair spray to hold your final style.
HP505	Conditioner	9544	3.45	
HP506	Mousse	9545	2.45	
HP507	Hair gel	9546	2.45	
HP508	Hair spray	9547	3.00	

* All these prices are approximate depending on the brands used.

Exam Practice 3 Document 4

T

Please complete the Hair and Beauty form, and type an envelope or label to Miss Rebecca Dixon at the address below. Take two extra copies (on plain paper or photocopied) one for Head Beautician and one for file.

Address 14 Riverside Way
WARMINSTER
Wilts BA12 8DP

Telephone number 01985 2125652

She would like a full head perm and her choice is for a soft and lasting one.

She would also like to book the following treatments.

Basic facial massage including cleansing and toning.

A relaxing full body massage to include back, legs and arms.

Manicure and varnishing the nails.

4

Exam Practice 4 Document 1

T

Trafalgar Range ← Emphasise this heading

This brand new range of vehicles has four models. You are bound to find something that meets all your needs.

Check this detail with Document 2 and amend if necessary.

Included on all models is a fantastic range of equipment. Many of the items would be considered extras in other vehicle ranges.

These include:

Air bags
Central locking
Engine immobiliser
Electric sunroof
CD player
Luxury trim
Alloy wheels

Stereo/radio cassette
Electric windows
Alarm system
Power-assisted steering
Metallic paint
Air conditioning

Sort into exact alphabetical order and type in one column.

The stylish new designs make these vehicles fun to drive. They are all very economical to run. Don't take our word for it – come and test drive the model of your choice today!

Change vehicle to car throughout this document.

Exam Practice 4 Document 2

T

BUYING A NEW CAR

Next month the new car registration will be issued. If you are thinking of buying a new car then visit us to see the latest models. Wrighton Motors are dealers of Nixon cars, the first name in British-made vehicles.

Nixon is celebrating 25 years of making quality cars by launching a brand-new family range. Wrighton Motors are pleased to announce the arrival of these models at their showrooms.

The Trafalgar range includes the following models.

Centre this line

£8,500	Phoebe PH4
£18,500	Nile N17
£12,650	Hero HE2
£10,990	Helena HE4
£14,500	Leander LE6

Sort into exact price order and display the names as the first column.

Leave a 5.1cm (51mm) gap here

Modify the layout so that the headings are on a separate line to the text, ie

The Phoebe

This is a hatchback . . . . .

The Phoebe – This is a hatchback with a difference. Compact and easy to drive, it is surprisingly spacious inside. The Phoebe is perfect for driving around town. The school run

4

is much more fun in a Phoebe. It comes in two models, petrol and diesel. Whichever you choose, it is very economical to drive.

The Helena – A family-sized saloon car which is perfect for longer journeys. Smart and stylish, its interior is remarkably comfortable. Included as standard is a range of extras that rival many other much more expensive cars.

The Hero – This sporty GTI has been designed for those who love the open road. The Hero is powerful but easy to handle. It comes in a range of fashionable colours. A soft-top convertible model is also available.

The Leander – An estate car that will suit all your needs. Whether you are stocking up at the supermarket or taking the family on holiday, you will have plenty of room in this spacious car. Petrol or diesel, manual or automatic, the Leander has a model for you.

The Nile – With this multi-purpose vehicle you can seat 8 comfortably and still find room for the luggage. The seats can be arranged in a variety of positions. Days out are great fun in a Nile.

Visit Wrighton Motors this weekend and see this unique collection for yourself.

Exam Practice 4 Document 3

T

WRIGHTON MOTORS

(Rule as shown)

If you are looking for a used car than visit our showrooms. We have a large range of used cars in all price ranges. We are sure you will find something to suit your needs. Buying from Wrighton Motors gives you the assurance that your new car will prove to be reliable and in top condition. All our used cars have a one-year warranty.

Below is a selection of the used cars we currently have on offer.

Car Details		Description	Special Offers*	
Make	Year		Trade Price**	Our Price
Pearl Chiltern BWD 934 Fifi Pearl	J L M P G	Hatchbacks Perfect as a run-around, hatchbacks suit the smaller family or as a second car.	£4,500 £5.000 £5,400 £6,750 £3,200	£4,250 £4,600 £5,150 £6,525 £3000
Malvern Chloe Sapphire BWD 964 Chloe	P K F N D	Saloons These family cars are excellent value. Many come with power-assisted steering, central locking and stereo radio/cassette.	£11,500 £7,500 £5,500 £9,500 £4,500	£11,200 £7,350 £5,250 £8,999 £4,000
Diamond Buxton Chantel BWD984 Diamond	M K L J H	Estates We have a large range of estate cars. Manual or automatic, these spacious vehicles are suitable for a variety of uses.	£14,000 £11,500 £12,999 £9,999 £8,750	£13,250 £11,200 £12,650 £9,480 £8,500

* These special offers are for a limited period only

** Trade prices quoted for January 1997.

4

Exam Practice 4 Document 4

T

Please complete the Wrighton Motors form. Take 2 extra copies, one for Martin Petty and one for the file.

Name and address:

Mr David Hill
17 Apsley Road
PORTSMOUTH
PO6 9ZZ

Telephone 01823 624491

David is interested in the following cars

Uk Motors	Malvern	£10,000 – £12,000
Beavais Cars	Chloe	£8,000 – £9,500

He is interested in interest-free finance, however David does not want to go on the mailing list.

Date for today.

Please type an envelope or label to

Wrighton Motors
Drake Street
PORTSMOUTH
PO9 8JK

Letterheads, memo forms and blank pre-printed forms for photocopying

The letterheads, memos and blank pre-printed forms which follow are for use throughout this book and may be photocopied. As there are two letterheads shown on one page ensure that you cover up the letterhead not needed with a blank sheet of paper when photocopying.

world ecology forum

Unit 2 Selbourne Way
Park Trading Estate
READING
Berks RG7 6LU

Phone 01827 3892888 Fax 01827 3832777

E79 3BE
LONDON
189 Fulham Mews
AQUA ART GALLERY

Craft Fayre

23 High Street
HAVERFORDWEST
Pembs
HV17 8BW

Phone 01726 372910 Fax 01726 372911

Edwards & Partners
Estate Agents

75 Avon Way
The Moorings
BATH
BA1 3DL

Phone 01340 555111
Fax 01340 555222

The Art School

Hanley Way
GLASGOW
G72 8HN

Phone 01783 165238

Scenic Sites

47 Warwick Road
SOLIHULL
West Midlands
B90 8GF

Phone 01212 459621
Fax 01212 459622

Cornwall's Finest
Holiday Homes

48 High Street
TRURO
Cornwall
TR89 2NT

Phone 012723 838383 Fax 012723 8366692

MEMORANDUM

To

From

Ref

Date

RAILWAY EXHIBITION

BOOKING FORM

Name ....

Address ....

....

.... Postcode ....

Amount enclosed ....

Would you like to purchase the video of the Taunton to Minehead Line?

☐ Yes ☐ No

(Please insert an X in the appropriate box)

Please state family/single ticket*

Departure date and time	Short visits	Special instruction

Date ....

* Delete as appropriate

Bath Times Co Ltd

Unit 5 Charlestown Industrial Estate
TRING Herts HP23 8NE

Phone 01842 61430 Fax 01842 61342

Name ....

Address ....

.... Postcode ....

Telephone No (Day) .... (Eve) ....

Item	Quantity	Code No	Price per Item

I wish to pay by cheque/credit card*

I would like to be added to your mailing list : Yes ☐ No ☐

Date ....

* Delete as applicable

HAIR AND BEAUTY SALON

TREATMENT BOOKING FORM

Name ....

Address ....

....

.... Postcode ....

Telephone Number ....

☐ Full head perm ☐ Half head perm

(Please insert an X in the appropriate box)

Perm choice roller/soft and lasting*

Facial Treatment	Body Treatments	Nails

Date ....

* Delete as appropriate

WRIGHTON MOTORS

Drake Street
PORTSMOUTH
PO9 8JK

Phone: 01823 2838822

Details Request Form

Make	Model	Price Range

Would you like to receive details of our interest-free finance deals?

Yes ☐ No ☐

I would/would not like my name to be added to your mailing list*

Name ....

Address ....

.... Postcode ....

Telephone Number .... Date ....

* Delete as appropriate

Key to proof reading exercises

Proof Reading Practice Exercise 3

WP **T**

The Saxo Phones

1 this five-piece jazz band has just embarked on a nationwide tour. It will be playing at many venues throughout the country.

2 The Saxo Phones have a reputation for being a great live act.Their music is
3 guaranteed to make you swing.

Given below are some of the dates it will be playing in this area.

	Bath	1 April
	Bristol	3 April
4	Cheltnham	21 April
5	Swindon	4 May
	Yeovil	26 May
	Chippenham	27 May

6 Full details can be obtained from your local music store.   Look out for
7 advertisements in the local newSpaper. Tickets can be purchasedin advance for all
8 venues.

Come and swing with The Saxo Phones!

■ Errors

1 There needs to be a capital letter at the beginning of a sentence.

2 This paragraph has a ragged left-hand margin.

3 The space after the full stop has been omitted.

4 Cheltenham has been spelt incorrectly.

5 The date column for Swindon has not been aligned.

6 Too much space has been left after the full stop.

7 A capital appears in the middle of a word.

8 The space between purchased and in has been omitted.

Proof Reading Practice Exercise 4

WP **T**

Our ref SL/MA/62

8 August 1997

1 FOR THE ATTENTION OF __

Mr Stuart Lovell
Lovell Direct Marketing
9 Penn Lea Avenue
2 Milton Keynes
MK43 8BT
3 Dear Mr Lovell

4 Thank you for your recent letter setting out your terms of buisness.

5 I have now had the opportunity to discuss your terms with my collegues. I am pleased to inform you that we would like to purchase additional names and addresses for our mailing lists.

As you are aware, we are a toy company specialising in high quality, educational toys. We would be interested in purchasing the names of those who have young children in
6 the age range of 1-twelve years.

7 Please prepare a mailing list of 10,000 names and addresses in the format given on the attached specification. If possible, we would like to include these in our next mailing. This is due to go out on 12 September.

8 Please do not hesitate to contact me if you require any further iformation.

Yours sincerely

Mandy Atkins
Mail Order Manager

9 —

Errors

1 The attention line should include the name of the addressee.

2 The town has not been typed in capitals.

3 There is no clear line space between the address and the salutation.

4 The word business has been typed incorrectly.

5 The word colleagues has been typed incorrectly.

6 There is an inconsistent use of figures (both numbers and words have been used).

7 This paragraph has a ragged left-hand margin.

8 The word information has been typed incorrectly.

9 The enclosure has been omitted.

Proof Reading Practice Exercise 5

WP **T**

1 China and Glassware Department

We are having a clearance sale next week. The table below shows the ranges that are being discounted together with the sale prices.

2 Please ensure that the prices have been changed before the sale begins on Monday.

When customers purchase these items it should be pointed out that these ranges have been discontinued.

	Item	×Price £	Code No	Sale Price £
3				
	<u>Alice Range</u>			
	Dinner plate	5.50	AL9	4.00
	Cereal bowl	4.80	AL3	3.60
	Cup and saucer	8.90	AL8	7.50
4	Side plate	4.50	AL10	×3.00
	Serving plate	25.00	AL12	18.00
5	Crystal Range			
6				
	Large wine glass	6.00	CR41	4.00
	Small wine glass	5.00	CR48	3.50
	Champagne flute	8.00	CR31	5.50
7	Whisky tumbler	4.50	×CR45	3.00
	Liqueur glass	5.00	CR36	3.50
8	<u>Tessa Range</u>			
	Teapot	TE20	35.00	27.50
	Sugar bowl	TE25	10.50	8.00
	Milk jug	TE23	12.50	9.50
	Salad bowl	TE16	25.00	22.00
9	Butter dish	TE19	15.00	12.00
10				

■ Errors

1 The heading has not been emboldened.

2 A new paragraph has been started incorrectly.

3 The Price £ column is in the wrong place.

4 The 3.00 is out of line.

5 The Crystal Range has been typed in the wrong place.

6 The words Crystal Range have not been underlined.

7 The code CR45 should read CR44.

8 There is no clear space after the Crystal Range.

9 The sale price for the butter dish is incorrect.

10 The price £ column and code columns have been swopped on the Tessa Range.

WP T Exam Practice 1 Document 1

world ecology forum

Unit 2 Selbourne Way
Park Trading Estate
READING
Berks RG7 6LU

Our ref PW/CE

Date (date of typing)

FOR THE ATTENTION OF MR EDWARD JENKINS

Mighty Trees
Poplar Business Park
YORK
YO2 5JR

Dear Sirs

Thank you for your letter expressing interest in the conference we plan to run next year on the environment. I have noted that you will be willing to speak on trees and woodland issues in general.

Would you please ensure your talk gives information on our traditional trees. Oak, beech, hazel and ash should be included. You may wish to expand your talk on one of these species, for example the oak, explaining that it is one of our richest of natural habitats. Many birds nest in the oak. Wasps can lay eggs in young acorns. Butterflies can live high in the oak canopy.

We need to stress that our ancient woods and heritage are worth conserving, the various reasons why our woods have been destroyed and what the new challenges we face are. All this will make very interesting information for our delegates to hear.

I will be in touch with you again in the near future.

Yours faithfully

Paul Waterson
Conference Secretary

WP T Exam Practice 1 Document 2

MEMORANDUM

To Janet Parks

From Paul Waterson

Ref PW/CE

Date (date of typing)

We are getting a very good response from potential speakers for our conference on the environment. I attach a list of the replies received so far.

We need to analyse the list and ensure we have a good coverage of all aspects to do with the environment.

When we have done this we will have the opportunity to contact companies we feel are still needed to give us a balanced conference.

It may be necessary for us to contact specialist speakers for certain areas. So far we have had no response from anyone to talk about the ozone layer. I will keep you informed of how things are progressing on a weekly basis.

Enc

WP T Exam Practice 1 Document 3

SUBJECTS FOR CONFERENCE ON THE ENVIRONMENT

We have had confirmation from some speakers who are willing to talk on the following subjects. We need to have a complete draft of the conference by (give date).

<u>Recycling</u>

A lot of our household waste is buried on land. About half of this could be usefully recycled.

Recycling reduces the waste of raw materials and less energy is needed to produce new goods. Many authorities have prepared recycling plans.

Make use of the many collection points for glass, paper, metals, and other materials. Make your own compost from garden waste.

<u>In the home</u>

As well as saving you money, you can help lessen the threat of acid rain and global climate change by using energy more efficiently in the home.

Insulate your walls and fit thick loft insulation. Ensure all doors and windows are draught proof. Turn off all unused lights and appliances, especially televisions.

<u>In the garden</u>

Private gardens are important for providing food, water and shelter for birds and some wildlife. Do not use chemicals but try organic methods instead. Start a compost heap or use a compost bin.

Plant trees if you have room as they help to absorb excess carbon-dioxide. Do not burn anything other than woody garden waste on a bonfire.

<u>On the road</u>

All forms of transport cause air pollution through exhaust fumes. Use unleaded petrol if your car can take it. Take account of fuel economy and drive smoothly.

Walk, cycle or use public transport whenever you can. Even when a bus is only a quarter full it is twice as fuel efficient as a family car.

<u>Noise</u>

Noise can cause severe stress. Never underestimate the harmful effects of noise. It is the form of pollution which has the most immediate effect on people.

2

<u>Trees and woodland issues</u>

Trees produce oxygen, influence our weather and prevent soil erosion. They help to

filter dust, smoke and fumes within our towns and cities.

You can help us in the fight against pollution by planting more trees in your garden.

Join an organisation which is interested in preserving and building up our woodlands.

<u>In the countryside</u>

Always observe the country code and close gates, stay on public footpaths, and keep dogs under control. Do not pick or uproot any wild plants. Remember that wild plants and endangered animals are protected by law. There are over 160 species of plants protected under law.

<u>Rivers, lakes, beaches and drinking water</u>

Pollutants get into water through the drains and other discharges. Never put any left-over chemicals down the drain, toilet or in a stream.

We still need speakers on the greenhouse effect, and the ozone layer.

WP T Exam Practice 2 Document 1

AQUA ART GALLERY
189 Fulham Mews
LONDON
E79 3BE

Phone 01827 3892888   Fax 01827 3832777

Our ref RF/EH1/PB

(date of typing)

Mr Robert Frost
3A Dunsford Place
IPSWICH
Suffolk
IP39 1QQ

Dear Robert

I am delighted to inform you that the plans for your forthcoming exhibition at the Aqua Art Gallery are now taking shape.

As discussed, the exhibition will run for three weeks beginning on Friday 20 September. You will be expected to provide the exhibits one week in advance. This will allow plenty of time for setting up the exhibition.

A private viewing has been arranged for the Friday evening. This will take place in the Gallery from 7.00 pm to 8.30 pm. Wine and canapes will be served. Please let my secretary have the names and addresses of those you would like to invite. Please limit the number of guests to 20.

I am enclosing a sheet giving further details of our terms and conditions.

We look forward to a very successful partnership with you.

Yours sincerely

Patrick Beresford
Manager

Enc

WP T Exam Practice 2 Document 2

MEMORANDUM

To Faye Woods

From Patrick Beresford

Ref PB/FW/RFEH1

Date (date of typing)

URGENT

The dates of Robert Frost's exhibition have now been finalised. The private view has been arranged for Friday 20 September. This will take place from 7.00 pm to 8.30 pm.

As usual, wine and canapes will be served. I would be grateful if you could arrange for 3 local catering companies to provide some quotations. I believe there will be approximately 150 people attending this event. The food and wine must be of good quality. A budget of around £3.50 per head has been set. However, this figure may have to be increased.

The invitations will need to be printed soon. Please arrange for these to be designed. You will need to check with Toby as I believe he has already completed the front cover design.

Robert Frost will be letting you have a list of his guests. I have asked him to limit this to 20 people. You should have in your files a list of the guests who are usually invited to private viewings. Please check this is up to date and amend if necessary.

WP T

Exam Practice 2 Document 3

A GUIDE FOR EXHIBITORS

Holding an exhibition is a very exciting time. However, it can also be rather stressful. The success of the exhibition depends largely on its organisation. We aim to provide all the back-up required to make your exhibition as stress free and successful as possible. In order for us to provide this service, we need you to be aware of the following:

Deadlines

Whilst we realise it can be difficult to keep to deadlines they are very necessary to the smooth running of the exhibition. Please ensure that your work reaches the Gallery by the agreed date.

In order to make the most of your work, our staff need to have several days to plan the exhibition fully. If you do not provide your work on time, then an extra charge of 1% on all sales will be levied.

Layout

Our staff are very experienced in setting out exhibitions to their best advantage. Exhibitors are very welcome to come and view the setting up of their work. However, we would respectfully remind you that the contract gives us full control of the exhibition layout.

Commission

As agreed in our contract, the Gallery will take 20% commission on all sales. Although this may seem rather high, we would point out that this includes the cost of staffing the Gallery, the private view, catalogue and all publicity.

Any orders or commissions accepted through introductions made at the Gallery are also subject to a 20% fee.

Catalogue

A full-colour catalogue will be prepared on behalf of the Gallery. This will be produced at the Gallery's expense. The design, copy and layout will be controlled by the Gallery. The copyright will be assigned to Aqua Art Gallery. In order to ensure that the information given is completely accurate, it will be the responsibility of the artist to check the copy.

2

Pricing

It is hoped that the price of the exhibits will be agreed between the exhibitor and the Gallery. The Gallery has a great deal of experience in this area and can give realistic advice.

Private View

This is a very important occasion as art critics, dealers and buyers attend. Please ensure you are available for this event and are prepared to be interviewed by the press.

Payment

Payment for work sold will be made by cheque no later than 28 days after the closing date of the exhibition. Any commission fees will be deducted before payment is made.

We hope that your exhibition is very successful.

WP T Exam Practice 3 Document 1

Craft Fayre
23 High Street
HAVERFORDWEST
Pembs
HV17 8BW

Phone 01726 372910 Fax 01726 372911

Our ref EV/PM/192

(date of typing)

Ms Ella Vaughan
Rose Cottage
DRUIDSTONE
Pembs
PB82 3NE

Dear Ms Vaughan

Thank you for your recent letter and photographs of your craft work. I have now had the opportunity to discuss your work with my colleagues. We believe we will be able to sell your jewellery through our craft shop.

I would be grateful if you could make an appointment to see me. May I suggest Thursday of next week, (give date). Please ring my assistant, Josie Walters to arrange a convenient time. Please bring samples of your jewellery.

If your work is accepted we would expect you to be able to keep your area fully stocked throughout the year.

A commission of 30% is taken from all sales of your work to cover the shop overheads. Orders for work taken through the shop are also subject to the commission payment.

I look forward to meeting you.

Yours sincerely

Peter Marshall
Manager

WP T Exam Practice 3 Document 2

MEMORANDUM

To Josie Walters

From Peter Marshall

Ref JW/PM/EV

Date (date of typing)

URGENT

I am enclosing a copy of a letter from Ella Vaughan, together with some photographs of her work. I believe the jewellery is just what we are looking for to fill the space we have now Graham has left. As you will see, I have asked Ms Vaughan to contact you to make an appointment. I can meet her at any time on Thursday.

Last week I left you a leaflet to type and have printed. Have you been able to do this yet? I would be grateful if you could make this a priority. We need to have the leaflet ready for the start of the tourist season. Please let me have a draft copy to check before you take it to the printers. We should have approximately 500 printed to start with. Please telephone 3 printers to find out the cost.

Encs

WP T

Exam Practice 3 Document 3

CRAFT FAYRE

Craft Fayre sells hand-made goods made by local craftspeople. The shop is ideally placed for the tourist trade and is building a reputation amongst local people for its unusual and beautiful gifts.

There is a large range of gifts on sale including jewellery, hand-knitted garments, clocks, ceramics, paintings and silk scarves. The Craft Fayre is always searching for new and interesting items. This means the range changes regularly.

Among the regular contributors to the Craft Fayre are:

Katy Medworth

Katy is a silk-screen printer. On sale at the Craft Fayre is a range of her silk scarves and greeting cards. The limited edition designs for her silk scarves are both unusual and eye-catching. The range of greeting cards is suitable for any occasion.

Samantha Jacobs

Samantha is a watercolour expert. Her paintings of local places of interest and landscapes are very popular. She has exhibited at many galleries throughout the country and studied at St Martin's School of Art.

Ryan Dolman

Mirrors and picture frames are Ryan's speciality. They are hand-painted with bright, modern designs. If you have a particular design in mind, Ryan will be delighted to make a frame to your own specification. These make excellent gifts.

Ricky Thompson

Ricky makes the most exquisite leather goods. Handbags, belts, purses and briefcases form his range. The designs are unique and the goods are beautifully made. Only the best quality leather is used.

Mary Lovell

Hand-knitted garments in every colour and style can be found in Mary's display of goods. A variety of yarns are used including wool, cashmere, cotton and silks.

Max Hanson

Clocks of all types and sizes are Max's speciality. Max has been making clocks for many years and uses a variety of materials. These beautiful timepieces will become heirlooms to be handed down the generations.

Nicholas Millard

The wonderful range of pottery Nicholas produces is modern and colourful. His work is fun and practical. Each item is sold separately so you can start your collection straightaway.

Oliver Sinclair

Hand-crafted furniture made from pine is Oliver's trade. A small range of cupboards and chairs can be seen at the Craft Fayre. Larger pieces such as wardrobes, beds and dressers can be seen at Oliver's workshop.

Freya Andrews

Freya designs and makes clothes especially for young children. They are made in 100% cotton and are easy to wash. Children love the bright colours and modern designs. At very reasonable prices, these are always popular with our customers.

We look forward to seeing you soon.

WP T Exam Practice 4 Document 1

Edwards & Partners
Estate Agents

75 Avon Way
The Moorings
BATH
BA1 3DL

Phone 01340 555111
Fax 01340 555222

Our ref JE/398

(Date of typing)

PRIVATE

Mr and Mrs T Knowles
49 Town Street
COVENTRY
CV2 3RP

Dear Mr and Mrs Knowles

With reference to your letter concerning the purchase of a luxury apartment in Bath. I am delighted to hear that you have decided to retire to Bath and as you are both over 50 years of age, all requirements for the Avon View apartments are fulfilled.

I would like to confirm the following details. The apartment you have chosen is on the third floor on the front of the building overlooking Bath Abbey. Features include a private dining salon, lounge, library, gymnasium, sauna, roof garden, two lifts, security and underground garage parking. In addition to these features, there is also a guest suite available.

I understand you will be visiting Bath this weekend. Our offices are open all day Saturday and I look forward to meeting you again. We can then proceed with the next phase of the purchase.

Yours sincerely

John Edwards
Sales Negotiator

WP T Exam Practice 4 Document 2

MEMORANDUM

To Amanda Longman

From John Edwards

Ref JE/398

Date (Date of typing)

I refer to our recent staff meeting concerning the sale of the Avon View apartments in Bath. I have now prepared a report on this and a copy is attached for your information.

We need to launch a fresh advertising campaign to ensure that all these apartments are sold by the end of the year. Can you please make this a priority? Traditionally properties sell well during March and April but so far this year this has not been the case.

You will need to emphasise the beauty of the city and all the amenities that are to hand for the over 50s. As these apartments are aimed at the retirement market, use security as a selling aid. Stress the fact that there is a central system controlling access to the building.

Enc

WP T Exam Practice 4 Document 3

AMENITIES IN BATH

The following amenities should be used in any future advertising campaign.

Bath is one of the most fascinating cities in the country. It is also one of the easiest to explore. It has a compact centre of broad main streets linked by quaint, narrow and traffic-free lanes. Elegant crescents and terraces of pale gold stone greet the eye around every corner.

<u>Although the city is surrounded by hills the walking is relatively flat in the city itself. Ideal for those lazy days of retirement.</u>

<u>Walks</u>

Step out of Avon View apartments and you have a wide choice of walks. You can walk along the River Avon and see the famous Pulteney Bridge which is lined with shops on both sides.

<u>Views</u>

You have a wonderful view of the weir - lean over the parapet and watch the activity below. Pleasure boats filling up, swimmers risking their lives near the weir and canoeists bobbing about everywhere.

<u>Flowers</u>

Orange Grove is immediately on your doorstep. The trees and flowers in spring and summer are a picture to behold. Bath has won the 'Britain in Bloom' contest so many times that nowadays it is only allowed to enter every other year. Alongside Orange Grove you have Parade Gardens where you can sit and listen to a band concert being played from the band stand.

<u>History</u>

Some apartments on the front of the building have a magnificent view of Bath Abbey. The 15th century abbey is in the very heart of the city and when floodlit at night is a spectacular sight. The interior is very light and is famous for its soaring traceries of fan-vaulting.

If you are interested in history, Bath has many museums for you to visit. These include the Museum of Costume, the Carriage Museum and the Museum of Bookbinding to name just a few.

2

The Assembly Rooms are not far away whilst the Guildhall is next door to the apartments.

The Guildhall has an 18th century banqueting room complete with many beautiful chandeliers. Part of the Guildhall complex houses a small market where you can just browse or buy anything from food to antiques.

You will be within a few minutes' walk of the Roman Baths, the perfect place to take your guests when they come to visit you. The therapeutic value of the spa still remains today. Alongside the baths is the Pump Room. Afternoon tea here is a must.

<u>General</u>

There is an excellent theatre, sports centre with swimming pool and many restaurants close at hand. Bath is also well-known for its fine shops.

It is necessary for me to see your rough draft of the advertising by (give date).

WP Exam Practice 1 Document 1

GOOD IDEAS!

HOME DECORATION

If you are looking to brighten up your house why not try some different paint effects. These are quick, easy and inexpensive but can make a great difference to your home. You do not have to be a talented artist as these effects are easy to do.

There are many good books for sale which give full details of these techniques. Your local DIY store may also offer help and advice.

Colourwashing - This has a subtle effect which adds colour and tone. It is good for covering uneven plasterwork.

Apply two base coats of emulsion paint with a roller. Allow to dry thoroughly. When dry, apply a coat of colourwash using criss cross strokes. Vary the angle of the strokes to show the base coat underneath.

When this coat has dried, you will be able to see if there are any areas that are uneven. Now apply a second coat. Try to make the strokes cross the first coat strokes at right angles

Stencilling - This is simple to do but very effective. Stencil kits containing paints, brushes and stencils are available at art shops and DIY stores. If you are more adventurous you can easily make your own designs using strong card or acetate.

GOOD IDEAS!

Stippling - To achieve this effect you paint a layer of glaze over your base colour. Then using a stipple brush, you break up the colour into a series of dots which when dry gives a texture rather like airbrushing. Anyone can do this and the results look very professional.

Apply two coats of base colour using eggshell paint. When this has dried you can apply the glaze in strips. Let this dry a little. Now using a stipple brush dipped in colour, stab the wall at right angles so that the colour breaks up into the glaze. If you are using this effect in a kitchen or bathroom, you may need to apply a coat of clear varnish.

Sponging - This gives a mottled effect and can look very attractive. You will need a small sea sponge to achieve this effect.

After applying two coats of base colour, allow to dry thoroughly. Pour a little paint in a tray and dab the sponge in. Squeeze the sponge gently to remove excess paint. Now, dab the wall with the sponge in a random direction. Change the direction of the sponge occasionally to get a speckled effect.

When this has dried, follow these steps again using a toning colour.

There are many good books for sale which give full details of these techniques. Your local DIY store may also offer help and advice.

2

GOOD IDEAS!

There are also a number of courses and workshops available. Find out if your local college has any courses on offer.

3

WP Exam Practice 1 Document 2

The Art School

Home Decoration Workshops

If you are tired of your decorations but cannot afford the services of a professional decorator, why not try do-it-yourself? It is much easier than you would think. By applying some different paint effects you can achieve very professional results.

The Art School offers one-day workshops on the various paint techniques. The following will be held over the next three months.

Colourwashing
Marbling
Rag Rolling
Sponging
Stenciling
Stippling

The workshop fees include refreshments and a buffet lunch. Please bring some protective clothing.

For further information and/or an enrolment form, please contact:

Jennifer MacDonald
The Art School
Hanley Way
GLASGOW
G72 8NH

Telephone 01783 162538.

WP T Exam Practice 1 Document 3

To All Staff

Home Decoration Workshops

Please note that the following workshops have been arranged. The course leaders should check with the Admissions Secretary a week before the workshop that enough students have enrolled. Please ensure that you have plenty of materials ordered in advance.

The refreshments will be served in the Green Room. Lunch will be at 12.30 pm.

Course	Course Leader	Date	Time
June Workshops			
Sponging	Frank Powell	3 June	9.30 am - 4.00 pm
Stencilling	Tracey Hull	6 June	11.00 am - 4.00 pm
Stippling	Shirley Davies	8 June	9.00 am - 4.00 pm
Colourwashing	Alyssa Marks	21 June	10.00 am - 3.00 pm
July Workshops			
Sponging	Fiona Harper	3 July	10.15 am - 4.00 pm
Marbling	Chris Middleton	4 July	9.00 am - 4.00 pm
Stencilling	Peter Hamilton	19 July	9.30 am - 3.00 pm
Rag rolling	Sam McFee	25 July	10.00 am - 3.00 pm
August Workshops			
Marbling	Eddie Fryer	2 August	11.00 am - 5.00 pm
Rag rolling	Moira Bailey	11 August	10.00 am - 3.00 pm
Stippling	Chris Middleton	12 August	9.30 am - 3.30 pm
Colourwashing	John Somerset	19 August	10.00 am - 3.45 pm

WP Exam Practice 1 Document 4

The Art School
Hanley Way
GLASGOW
G72 8HN

Phone 01783 165238

Our ref PW/MW/HDC

(date of typing)

Mrs Penny Whitmarsh
7 King's Road
GLASGOW
G27 2NK

Dear Mrs Whitmarsh

Thank you for your completed enrolment form and cheque. I confirm you have been allocated a place on the Sponging Workshop on 3 June. A copy of this letter will be sent to Frank Powell, who is the course leader.

The workshop will take place at The Art School's main building in Hanley Way. Please come to Studio 15 which is on the second floor. A lift is available for disabled students.

Refreshments are included in the workshop fee. These include a buffet lunch and coffee. If you require a special diet, please let us know at least 2 days in advance.

All materials are also included in the fee. However you will need to bring some protective clothing. An opportunity to purchase the special equipment required will be available at the end of the day. This equipment includes paint brushes, sponges, rollers, etc.

We look forward to meeting you and hope you enjoy your day.

Yours sincerely

Marsha Wilmot
Admissions Secretary

Copies Frank Powell
File

Copies Frank Powell
File

Copies Frank Powell
File

WP Exam Practice 2 Document 1

SCENIC SITES

TOURING CARAVAN HOLIDAYS

Before you start your holiday you must ensure your caravan has been serviced regularly so that it is safe in all respects when touring on the road and when on site. As an extra to the normal service, have the body checked for signs of damp. It is a good idea to have this done early in the year before your first trip.

Firstly check your caravan tyre pressures, including the spare, and wheel-nut tightness. Turn off the gas cylinder and make sure it is strapped upright.

Empty all water tanks and carry any water required for your journey in a small container in the car. Secure any loose items in the caravan, close windows and rooflights. Fasten travel catch on refrigerator and cupboards.

You will need to check the noseweight of the caravan. The recommended figure will be in your handbook. Ensure your handbrake is fully on and then raise corner steadies and stow winding handle and step. Lock the door.

SCENIC SITES

Many people now wear gloves to protect their hands when doing these outdoor chores.

You can now hitch your caravan on to your towing vehicle. Clamp the jockey wheel securely in place and fit stabiliser if used.

Connect wiring cables and check all lights and indicators are working. Fit extension wing mirrors for a better view when towing. Walk round the caravan for a final check.

When you have been towing for about 20 minutes stop and walk round the caravan again. Check that all the windows are still fastened and that everything looks secure inside.

For safety reasons we recommend you carry a 1 kg dry powder extinguisher. A fire blanket is advisable for the kitchen area and also a smoke detector.

If you are going to use a trailer tent or an awning as a cooking area it is wise to have a large bucket of water handy when sited. This is in addition to the fire extinguisher and fire blanket.

2

SCENIC SITES

You will need to check the noseweight of the caravan. The recommended figure will be in your handbook. Ensure your handbrake is fully on and then raise corner steadies and stow winding handle and step. Lock the door.

On arrival at your site check in first with the owner or warden. Be sure to follow instructions given by them for siting your caravan. In order to make sure your refrigerator operates properly level the caravan to within 3 degrees.

After you are safely settled on a pitch fit the hitchlock and wheel clamp to secure your caravan. You now deserve that welcome cup of tea!

3

WP Exam Practice 2 Document 2

CARAVAN INSURANCE COVER

We can arrange insurance cover for your caravan, your car or motor caravan. Our premiums are very favourable and we can provide the insurance you personally need.

If you travel abroad in Europe we can provide free foreign travel cover provided your journey does not exceed 31 days. For motor caravan drivers up to 3 months' cover is provided. Special arrangements can be made for longer periods.

Our motor caravan foreign travel covers the following.

Aerials
Awnings
Baggage
Batteries
Cassette players
Heaters
Radios
Television
Toilet tents
Water carriers

Our most popular insurance choice includes comprehensive cover on or off the road. It's a new for old cover with caravan age restriction of up to 5 years old. Your caravan contents are also covered. You can have automatic cover for use of your caravan by family and friends.

We also have a special travel service insurance especially for caravaners. This gives motoring, medical, baggage and personal cover as a package deal.

Our claims service is fast and fair.

WP Exam Practice 2 Document 3

CARAVAN HOLIDAY SITES

BRITISH SITES		NUMBER OF PITCHES	AREA IN ACRES
COUNTY OR REGION	NAME OF SITE		
England			
Cornwall	Four Ways	70	4
Devon	Flower Corner	120	7
Somerset	Five Arches	135	9
Dorset	Cross Hill	150	25
Essex	The Grove	180	12
Hampshire	Wood Park	185	15
Kent	South Oak	190	17
Cumbria	High Park	200	20
Wales			
Powys	Owl Tree	30	3
Clwyd	Lady Anne	35	2
Dyfed	Shaw Country	50	4
Gwent	Sunshine Way	55	5
Gwent	Low Park	60	5
Dyfed	The Lake	70	4
Powys	Forest Walk	90	8
Scotland			
Grampian	Golden Bank	55	4
Central	Blair Way	90	8
Fife	Mountain Way	110	8
Highland	The Moor	120	8
Highland	Riverbank View	150	23
Lothian	The Gardens	155	15

Site opening times, facilities and prices vary. Many sites are now open all year. There is usually a dog walk on site or nearby and dogs must be on a lead at all times.

WP Exam Practice 2 Document 4

Scenic Sites

47 Warwick Road
SOLIHULL
West Midlands
B90 8GF

Phone 01212 459621
Fax 01212 459622

Our ref DA/WD

Date (Date of typing)

Mr and Mrs A Stone
153 Princess Street
WAKEFIELD
West Yorkshire
WF1 6PQ

Dear Mr and Mrs Stone

WARDENS AT GOLDEN BANK SITE

Thank you both for attending our training day last week. I am pleased to offer you the post of Wardens at the above site for the coming season.

The site is situated in a most beautiful part of Scotland. Would you please visit it within the next week and let me have your decision as to whether you will accept the post. Your post will commence on 1 March and end on 31 October and the site is open to caravaners from 31 March to 3 October.

Throughout March you will have time to get the site ready after the winter for visitors. Hedges will need trimming and grass cut if dry enough. You will know from past experience the type of jobs that are needed to be done.

Likewise the month of October is used to close the site down for the winter months. There is always a lot of work to be done after a busy summer season.

The site will open this year with more hardstanding pitches and the play area has been extended.

A full list of duties and responsibilities for the post will be sent to you on receipt of your acceptance.

Yours sincerely

David Armstrong
Personnel Officer

cc Sites Manager
File

cc Sites Manager ✓
File

cc Sites Manager
File ✓

WP Exam Practice 3 Document 1

Letting your Property

Cornwall's Finest Holiday Homes

This leaflet aims to tell you about our letting agency and to give you information on how to turn your holiday home into a successful business.

We are a long-established letting agency concentrating on homes in Cornwall. Each year we produce a full-colour brochure featuring over 350 homes to let.

The full-colour brochure features a photograph of every property together with professionally written details, making it interesting and easy to read. We receive over 45,000 enquiries each year.

Our experience in this business means that we can give an expert opinion as to the potential of your holiday property. We can also advise you on the amount of rent you can realistically expect to receive.

By choosing us as your letting agent you can be assured you will receive a first-class service. Our competent staff deal with all the details on your behalf. They provide a friendly and efficient service. Our offices are open from 9.30 am to 6.30 pm 7 days a week. This means you will never miss an opportunity for letting your home.

As we deal with many properties our commission charges are extremely reasonable. A basic rate of 15% plus VAT is payable for each letting. A yearly charge of £75 is also payable for the Tourist Board inspection. If you are registered for VAT you may claim back the VAT payable on commission.

The Tourist Board has an inspection service that grades holiday properties on a scale of 1 to 5. This is assessed on a yearly basis and offers peace of mind to our customers. They must be able to rely on the property they book to be comfortable and well-equipped. The assessment gives helpful feedback on making the most of your property. We do not accept properties that have a grading of less than 4.

We advise our property owners to take out cancellation insurance. This can be arranged through our offices. This means that should a holiday be cancelled because of accident or ill-health, etc, you will receive 85% of the usual price. You will also require Public Liability insurance for your property.

It is advised that you insure your home and contents against accidental damage by customers. Our agency has arranged a special deal with a local insurance company. It can offer you very reasonable rates for this service.

Letting your Property

You will probably wish to take some weeks for your family and friends. We ask you to limit this to four during the year. A maximum of two can be taken during the peak season. You do not have to let your home for the entire year. The minimum number of weeks is 24. A short break offer for the winter months is very popular with our customers. You may wish to consider this for your property.

We are a long-established letting agency concentrating on homes in Cornwall. Each year we produce a full-colour brochure featuring over 350 homes to let.

3

WP Exam Practice 3 Document 2

Cornwall's Finest Holiday Homes

<u>Inspection and Grading</u>

Holidaymakers expect high standards of quality and comfort when they book a property. Without a grading system, booking a property can be very hit or miss. Cornwall's Finest Holiday Homes will only accept properties that have undergone an inspection by the local tourist board. A grading of four or above must be attained.

In order for a property to obtain a high grade, it must be in excellent condition. The furniture and fittings must be of a high standard and free from wear and tear. The property must be clean and comfortable. Cleaning of the property between lettings must be undertaken.

Kitchens and bathrooms should be easy to clean and in good condition. Extra marks will be awarded for provision of the following items:

Automatic washing machine
Dishwasher
Freezer
Microwave oven
Tumble dryer

After the property has been inspected a full and detailed report will be written. This feedback is extremely useful in helping owners upgrade their homes.

WP Exam Practice 3 Document 3

Brochure Amendments

The following properties are now booked for the entire season. Please ensure the computer is updated. A letter will have to be sent to each of the owners informing them of this.

These properties are always very popular. We should consider featuring them on a separate page of the next brochure.

Address	Owner	Rental per Week £	Code
Penzance			
17 Willow Close	Eileen Jeffries	255	PS6
8 Castle Gardens	Colin Hynes	270	PS8
12 Selwood Drive	Ashley Griffin	295	PS13
23 Heron Court	Stanley Garland	320	PS2
1 The Slipway	Margaret Ashton	380	PS1
Truro			
82 High Street	Betty George	255	TR28
11 Chestnut Street	Karen Freeman	275	TR63
41 Mayfield Lane	Janice Wilson	280	TR6
28 Park Street	Neil Simmons	320	TR62
7 Woodlands Road	Jonathan Bridges	360	TR17
Portreath			
29 Eden Place	William Leeds	235	PR27
32 Harbour View	Matthew Palmer	295	PR5
6 Seaview Way	Peter Marks	340	PR32
Rose Cottage	Alice Scullin	365	PR12
Beach Cottage	Annabelle Rich	420	PR38

WP Exam Practice 3 Document 4

Cornwall's Finest
Holiday Homes

48 High Street
TRURO
Cornwall
TR89 2NT
Phone 012723 838383 Fax 012723 8366692

Our ref SVH/VJ/139

(date of typing)

Mrs Penny Whitmarsh
22 Westgate Street
HAYTON
Cumbria
CU27 3IN

Dear Mrs Whitmarsh

SEAVIEW HOUSE, ST IVES

The Tourist Board inspection report on your above property has now been received at our offices. A copy for your attention will be posted shortly. We are pleased to advise you that Seaview House has been awarded a Grade Four.

In view of this, we feel that a reasonable rent would be £340 per week. This rental will be reviewed at the end of the season. It may be that we can increase this by £50 per week for next season.

If you decide to place your property with our agency we will immediately produce a sheet to be included with our brochure. I am confident we can arrange many lettings for your holiday home this season.

I will need to have copies of insurance certificates for the property. A copy of this letter will be sent to Michael Ruskin, our insurance broker. He will contact you shortly.

If you require any further information please do not hesitate to contact me.

Yours sincerely

Colin Fraser
Manager

Copy Michael Ruskin
File

Copy Michael Ruskin ✓
File

Copy Michael Ruskin
File ✓

WP Exam Practice 4 Document 1

WILDLIFE FACT SHEET

A GARDEN FOR WILDLIFE

No matter how small your garden, with careful planning it can be a paradise for birds and other wildlife. A small pool is imperative as it makes a home for frogs and insects. It is also a place for birds to drink and bathe.

Build the pool with gently sloping sides. Have a stone wall close by for shelter for the frogs and toads.

Plant a few shrubs that have berries as these make natural food for birds. They also give winter food for all kinds of small creatures.

> Although a Bhuddleia shrub can grow quite tall its blooms attract many different butterflies.

Blackbirds and thrushes find a lawn a perfect feeding ground. The song thrush has a fine voice and sings for much of the year. The robin is a frequent visitor to almost all gardens. You cannot fail to see him with his bright orange-red face and breast.

WILDLIFE FACT SHEET

Listen for spring being heralded at both dawn and dusk by the blackbird's song. These birds are perhaps our commonest of garden birds and nest in bushes.

Keep those precious autumn leaves and pile them under hedges and shrubs. Fill hedgehog boxes with them and put some in bin liners to rot down for use next year.

You are likely to find a wren poking among ground litter and picking food from the leaves. The wren has a tiny body but a loud voice, listen for its fast and shrill song.

Listen for spring being heralded at both dawn and dusk by the blackbird's song. These birds are perhaps our commonest of garden birds and nest in bushes.

From September think about bird feeding devices. Small birds have to eat all day to survive the cold winter nights. The blue tit has very acrobatic feeding habits. Watch him feeding hanging upside-down on a nut holder.

Put your bird table and feeders close to the cover of a climbing plant or a

2

WILDLIFE FACT SHEET

shrub to give the birds shelter. Although you may not fancy a bath outside at this time of year, it is important for birds to have one. They bathe to keep their feathers in good condition. Replace frozen water in a bird bath each morning or float a ball in your pool to keep a small patch ice-free.

If you are keen on gardens and wildlife and would like to visit our organic gardens, send for our free booklet listing these. The best time to visit is June and July.

3

WP Exam Practice 4 Document 2

A POOL IN YOUR GARDEN

Water can be delightful in a garden. Its sight and sound are both relaxing and refreshing. The shape and size of a pool will depend on the site chosen for it. A generous rectangular, circular or oval shape is the most effective. If you have a large garden a more irregular shape to form part of the natural landscape would be more in character.

We will be running a series of courses on how to design and construct a pool. Instruction will be given on how to measure up and landscape the site, suitable materials and methods of construction.

The design course dates are as follows.

6 September 1997
10 September 1997
13 September 1997
27 September 1997
8 October 1997
18 October 1997

The design course will begin with coffee and registration at 10.30 am. Bring your own packed lunch, and drinks will be provided. You will need a notebook, a pad of drawing paper, recommended size A3, and suitable drawing instruments and pencils. The day will close with tea and biscuits at 4 pm.

WP Exam Practice 4 Document 3

WILDLIFE GARDEN COURSES

STUDENT REGISTRATION DETAILS		TYPE OF COURSE	ROOM NUMBER
NAME	NUMBER		
6 September - 18 October (Pools)			
BARNES D	012	Design	4
CARTER G	006	Planting	8
DAY A	019	Construction	7
SCOTT L	037	Design	4
SMEDLEY C	004	Construction	7
TURNER F	030	Design	4
WALKER A	010	Planting	8
22 October - 8 November (Plants)			
ALLEN P	001	Trees	3
ELLISON A	009	Trees	3
HUNT D	024	Flowers	5
JONES W	017	Shrubs	1
KNIGHT H	032	Flowers	5
PARSONS D	015	Shrubs	1
12 November - 29 November (Hard Features)			
McDONALD S	002	Paving	2
RICHARDS M	020	Fencing	6
STENNER R	014	Building	9
STRINGER A	035	Building	9
WILLIAMS S	036	Paving	2
YOUNG K	033	Fencing	6

All the above courses are now full and a waiting list is being kept. They have all paid the minimum fee of £25 for the day.

WP Exam Practice 4 Document 4

MEMORANDUM

To All Course Leaders

From Caroline Brook

Ref CB/WGC

Date (Date of typing)

You will see from the attached list that all places are now fully booked for the autumn series. We have compiled a waiting list and this will be used in strict order of registration should a place become available.

The course on pool construction will take place partly in room 7 and partly outside in the workshop area. Students have been asked to wear suitable clothes and footwear.

On 26 October the tree course will be held in room 4 as room 3 is being decorated that weekend. Students will be informed of this change at registration.

All the courses on hard features in the garden will have the necessary theory in the rooms allocated. The rest of the time will be spent outside doing practical work.

Please ensure you have enough materials you will all respectively need for the courses. We have always had a high standard of efficiency and would like to maintain this.

Courses will start promptly at 10.45 am and a lunch break will be taken from 1 pm to 1.45 pm in the canteen area where drinks will be provided. Tea and biscuits will end the day at 4 pm and will again be served in the canteen area.

Please let me have a copy of the contents of your course for our records.

Enc

cc Site Administrator
File

cc Site Administrator ✓
File

cc Site Administrator
File ✓

T Exam Practice 1 Document 1

RAIL STEAM TOURS

Following the success of our last steam tours we are pleased to give you details of a new tour we are adding to our list this year.

This will take place through the West Country from Taunton to Minehead. You will travel through country stations viewing thatched cottages along the way. At Watchet your route is alongside the harbour, and you will see Dunster Castle before arriving at Minehead station on the sea front.

The tours will take place on the following dates.

1	June
4	June
15	June
18	June
6	July
9	July
13	July
20	July
3	August
6	August
10	August
13	August

BE SURE TO VISIT OUR RAILWAY EXHIBITION WHILST IN MINEHEAD.

T Exam Practice 1 Document 2

MINEHEAD RAILWAY EXHIBITION

The exhibition is open on all tour dates from 10 am to 5 pm. It is run by volunteer stewards who will be very happy to answer any questions you may have.

A snack bar will be open serving a selection of drinks and light meals. There will also be a number of trade stands selling models, books, calendars, art prints and video tapes. Choose from the following list a video tape of your favourite railways to take home and remember your day out.

Diesel locos	Rails through the sand
Electric trains	Rocket to Eurostar
Glasgow tramcar	Rolling stock
Great Western	Royal Scot 2
Light rail	Signalling
Lost railways	Stations
North Devon line	Steam locos
Past and present	

To go with this tour, take advantage of our special offer video tape of the Taunton to Minehead line. This offer is only available to tour ticket holders.

The following details are given as a guide to the exhibits.

<u>Minster Junction</u>

This is a single-track branch line which is joined at Minster Junction by another single-track line from Johnson Wharf. The layout is mainly hand built and the rolling stock is kit built.

T Exam Practice 1 Document 3

MODEL RAILWAYS SALE

Visit our stands at the exhibition in Minehead and browse through our sale stock. We are sure you will find a bargain.

Description of models		Class and price		Stand Information
Code Number	Type	Name	£	
A142	Steam	Branchline	50.50	On stand numbers 7-9 you will find a variety of train sets all of which include locos, rolling stock, power unit and a circle of track. All items are boxed as a set.
A143	Diesel	Freight	52.50	
A144	Steam	Pullman	96.50	
A145	Electric	Intercity	70.80	
A146	Diesel	Night Mail	87.15	
A147	Steam	Coronation*	80.50	
B237	Steam	Mallard	53.70	A wide range of locos is displayed on stands 5 and 6. Most models are on sale in the colours of the new train companies.
B238	Steam	Saint	45.50	
B239	Diesel	Deltic	33.50	
B240	Diesel	Western	34.50	
B241	Electric	Southern	30.50	
B242	Electric	Express	34.35	
C362	Goods	Hopper	5.95	For a full range of rolling stock visit stands 1 and 2. Coaches are available in most train company colours. Goods wagons are priced singly but a discount will be given for bulk orders.
C363	Goods	Tank	4.80	
C364	Goods	Grain	6.50	
C365	Coach	Dining	10.20	
C366	Coach	Intercity	12.20	
C367	Coach	Pullman	12.50	

* This model is only available while stocks last.

2

Great Bar Goods

This goods yard is set in the Midlands during the changeover from steam to diesel. The layout is constructed on a single board complete with track and points.

Eastmoor

This is a small layout built to be usable in a modern house. The locos are mainly diesels from the 1950s through to the present day.

Edwards Green

Setting the scene for this layout, summer is long gone and the harvest is gathered in. One captures the feeling of a small Devon station serving a village and farming community.

Throughout the day there will be various demonstrations of model and kit making skills.

T Exam Practice 1 Document 4

RAILWAY EXHIBITION

BOOKING FORM

Name ...Mr Andrew Miller...

Address ...3 Raglans Lane...

...SWINDON...

...Wilts.................. Postcode ...SN2 2LP..................

Amount enclosed ...£25.00...

Would you like to purchase the video of the Taunton to Minehead Line?

[X] Yes   [ ] No

(Please insert an X in the appropriate box)

Please state ~~family~~/single ticket*

Departure date and time	Short visits	Special instruction
9.15 am on 6 August	Loco repair workshop and museum at Washford and the old town harbour at Watchet.	Lineside photographer's permit.

Date ...(date of typing)...

* Delete as appropriate

cc Booking Clerk
   File

cc Booking Clerk ✓
   File

cc Booking Clerk
   File ✓

Rail Steam Tours
Wellington Road
TAUNTON
Somerset
TA1 4XJ

T Exam Practice 2 Document 1

BATH TIMES

Our new range of luxury bath accessories will be on sale at the end of January.

The Seaside range of toiletries will be in the shops in time for the summer holidays. In bright, stylish packaging with seaside motifs, the range is great fun. The familiar and fresh seaside fragrances will ensure your summer holiday stays with you throughout the year.

The range includes:

SEA420	Conditioner
SEA421	Bath foam
SEA422	Bath oil
SEA423	Hand and body lotion
SEA439	Shower gel
SEA463	Bath crystals
SEA464	Soap
SEA465	Talcum powder
SEA471	Shampoo

The Seaside collection costs from £1 for a luxury soap to £25 for a gift hamper full of goodies.

The Bath Times range is available from department stores or by mail order.

T Exam Practice 2 Document 2

Bath Times

The Bath Times Company sells high-quality bath accessories and goods. From soaps to bath towels, bathroom cabinets to shower curtains, you can find everything you need for your bathroom in our range.

Each year Bath Times produces several new collections of bath products. We are always updating our bath accessories' collections to match the latest in bathroom style.

We manufacture all our own toiletries. This way we can control production and ensure that the ingredients have not been tested on animals. All packaging is environmentally friendly. Where possible, the packaging is made from recycled materials.

Bath Times has been manufacturing bath products for over 20 years. It started as a small cottage industry supplying a local gift shop. Over the years it has grown and now supplies all the major department stores throughout the UK. A mail order service is available. A full-colour catalogue is published twice a year.

Our most popular range is the Country Collection which includes:

Bath crystals	Face wash
Bath foam	Hand cream
Bath oil	Moisturiser
Bath pearls	Shampoo
Body lotion	Shower gel
Body scrub	Soap
Conditioner	Talcum powder
Deodorant	Toner

2

All these products will be found in the new spring catalogue. This also features our latest collection, the Seaside range. It will be available on 24 January.

Included in the catalogue are the following:

Jungle Range - This range has been prepared especially for children. All products are made from the most mild ingredients. It is safe for children of all ages, including babies. The bright, well-designed packaging makes bath time fun. Children will love our exciting new additions to the range including a glitter bath foam and shower gel.

Just for Men - This fresh-smelling range of men's toiletries is very popular and is one of our best-selling collections. Products include aftershave, face wash and deodorant as well as the usual bath and shower items.

CALL 01842 61430 FOR A FREE COPY OF OUR CATALOGUE OR VISIT YOUR LOCAL DEPARTMENT STORE.

T Exam Practice 2 Document 3

Spring Catalogue Publicity Leaflet

The table below forms part of our new leaflet. This will contain colour photographs and an order form. The leaflet will be inserted in various, suitable magazines and newspapers. It is designed to promote the new spring catalogue.

Product details		Description	Catalogue details	
Item	Content		Price £	Code*
		Country Collection**		
Rose soap	100 gm	Fragrances of rose, lavender, carnation and lily of the valley are included in this range. Our best-selling items ever.	1.20	RS021
Rose bath oil	150 ml		2.50	RBO13
Rose hand cream	150 ml		1.75	RHC15
Rose shampoo	250 ml		2.35	RSH19
Rose conditioner	250 ml		2.50	RCR35
Rose shower gel	175 ml		2.50	RSG26
		Seaside Range		
Shower gel	225 ml	This fresh new range will remind you of long hot days by the sea. Suitable for all the family.	2.75	SEA439
Shampoo	250 ml		2.99	SEA471
Conditioner	250 ml		3.20	SEA420
Bath foam	175 ml		2.75	SEA421
Soap	240 gm		3.50	SEA464
		Jungle Range		
Zebra shampoo	150 ml	Children of all ages love this fun range of toiletries. The mild ingredients mean the products are suitable for babies.	1.85	JZS21
Lion bubble bath	280 ml		2.60	JLB23
Tiger shower gel	250 ml		2.30	JTS12
Hippo bath oil	230 ml		2.95	JHB38
Crocodile soap	120 gm		1.20	JCS28

* When ordering, please ensure you quote the correct code.
** These products are also available in Carnation, Lavender and Lily of the Valley fragrances.

T Exam Practice 2 Document 4

Bath Times Co Ltd
Unit 5 Charlestown Industrial Estate
TRING Herts HP23 8NE

Phone 01842 61430 Fax 01842 61342

Name Mr Simon Wing

Address 2 The Towers, BELFAST, Northern Ireland

Postcode BT3 4XY

Telephone No (Day) 01964 323195 (Eve) 01964 379882

Item	Quantity	Code No	Price per Item
Zebra Shampoo	1	JZS21	£1.85
Lion Bubble Bath	1	JLB23	£2.60
Crocodile Soap	1	JCS28	£1.20

I wish to pay by cheque/~~credit card~~*

I would like to be added to your mailing list : Yes [X] No [ ]

Date (date of typing)

* Delete as applicable

Copies Mrs Kathy Jones
File

Copies Mrs Kathy Jones ✓
File

Copies Mrs Kathy Jones
File ✓

Mrs Kathy Jones
22 Highland Grove
EDINBURGH
EH5 6XX

T Exam Practice 3 Document 1

YOUR SKIN AND YOUR TAN

When preparing for your holiday tan ensure you know about your skin type. We all like to get a healthy looking suntan but we forget the damage the sun can do to our skin.

If you have dark skin and dark hair your skin will usually tan easily but you still need protection from a sunscreen lotion or cream.

Choose from the following protections one to suit your own skin type.

12 Fair skin
13 Outdoor sports
14 Sunblock for face
15 In open cars
16 Maximum exposure
17 Normal skin
19 Dark skin
23 Around eyes
25 Total cover

<u>Apply a body lotion daily as part of your after sun care.</u>

T Exam Practice 3 Document 2

CARING FOR YOUR HAIR

Your hair is the frame for your face. To enhance your natural features your hair cut, style and condition are all very important. A shining head of hair makes you both look and feel good. You may have thick or fine hair, curly or straight, oily or dry but whatever it is you must give it the right care it needs daily.

When caring for your hair, ensure you observe the following.

Avoid rubbing when wet
Brush daily
Choose a good brush
Comb frequently
Condition often
Cut and style
Heated rollers
Little use of dryers
Shampoo gently
Thoroughly rinse
Wash brush and comb often
Wear gloves when colouring

HAIR CARE ROUTINE

To keep your hair clean you should wash it at least once a week. Wet hair with warm water and massage the shampoo gently into the hair and scalp. Experiment with different ones to discover the one that suits you best. Always rinse well and then repeat if your hair is very dirty or greasy.

CONDITION AND DRY

Massage the conditioner from the roots to the ends of the hair. Leave on as directed and then rinse the hair thoroughly. Brush your hair into style and leave to dry naturally or blow dry. Do not concentrate the heat in

2

one place and hold the drier at least 15 cm away from your hair.

STYLING

Your hairstyle can affect the shape of your face. It can create a new image for you and give you more confidence. Whatever style you choose it should be easy to look after and one you feel happy with. Visit your hairdresser once every six weeks to keep it in shape.

HAIR COLOUR

Most of us colour our hair at some time in our lives. The most natural colour for hair is only one or two shades darker or lighter than your own. Never dye your eyebrows and eyelashes.

Too much sun can damage your hair. Always wear a sun hat when out in the hot sun.

T Exam Practice 3 Document 3

SUMMER HOLIDAY SPECIAL

Take a break from your normal routine and give your skin and hair a fresh new feeling for the holiday season.

At Home and on Holiday		Product Cost*		General Comments
Reference	Item	Code Number	£	
SR302 SR303 SR304 SR305	Sun hat Sun glasses Sun cream Sun lotion	5136 5137 5138 5139	4.50 10.50 7.00 5.35	Make sure you and your family are protected with sun creams and lotions suitable for the country you are visiting.
BT401 BT402 BT403 BT404 BT405	Creme bath Shower creme Beauty soap Silk talc Bath mit	7221 7222 7223 7224 7225	3.50 3.50 2.75 2.50 4.75	For a relaxing bath ensure the water temperature is comfortably warm. A tepid bath helps you to unwind at the end of the day.
HP504 HP505 HP506 HP507 HP508	Shampoo Conditioner Mousse Hair gel Hair spray	9543 9544 9545 9546 9547	3.00 3.75 2.45 2.45 3.00	Use a conditioner to smooth the outer surface of the hair which is roughened by washing. Mist your hair with hair spray to hold your final style.

* All these prices are approximate depending on the brands used.

T Exam Practice 3 Document 4

HAIR AND BEAUTY SALON

TREATMENT BOOKING FORM

Name ...Miss Rebecca Dixon...

Address ...17 Riverside Way...

...WARMINSTER...

...Wilts... Postcode ...BA12 8DP...

Telephone Number ...01985 2125652...

[X] Full head perm [ ] Half head perm

(Please insert an X in the appropriate box)

Perm choice ~~rollor~~/soft and lasting*

Facial Treatment	Body Treatments	Nails
Basic facial massage including cleansing and toning.	A relaxing full body massage to include back, legs and arms.	Manicure and varnishing.

Date ...(date of typing)...

* Delete as appropriate

cc Head Beautician
File

cc Head Beautician ✓
File

cc Head Beautician
File ✓

Miss Rebecca Dixon
17 Riverside Way
WARMINSTER
Wilts
BA12 8DP

T Exam Practice 4 Document 1

TRAFALGAR RANGE

This brand new range of cars has five models. You are bound to find something that meets all your needs.

Included on all models is a fantastic range of equipment. Many of the items would be considered extras in other car ranges.

These include:

Air bags
Air conditioning
Alarm system
Alloy wheels
CD player
Central locking
Electric sunroof
Electric windows
Engine immobiliser
Luxury trim
Metallic paint
Power-assisted steering
Stereo/radio cassette

The stylish new designs make these cars fun to drive. They are all very economical to run. Don't take our word for it - come and test drive the model of your choice today!

T

Exam Practice 4 Document 2

BUYING A NEW CAR

Next month the new car registration will be issued. If you are thinking of buying a new car then visit us to see the latest models. Wrighton Motors are dealers of Nixon cars, the first name in British-made vehicles.

Nixon is celebrating 25 years of making quality cars by launching a brand-new family range. Wrighton Motors are pleased to announce the arrival of these models at their showrooms.

The Trafalgar range includes the following models:

Phoebe PH4	£ 8,500
Helena HE4	£10,990
Hero HE2	£12,650
Leander LE6	£14,500
Nile N17	£18,500

<u>The Phoebe</u>

This is a hatchback with a difference. Compact and easy to drive, it is surprisingly spacious inside. The Phoebe is perfect for driving around town. The school run is much more fun in a Phoebe. It comes in two models, petrol and diesel. Whichever you choose, it is very economical to drive.

<u>The Helena</u>

A family-sized saloon car which is perfect for longer journeys. Smart and stylish, its interior is remarkably comfortable. Included as standard is a range of extras that rival many other much more expensive cars.

2

<u>The Hero</u>

This sporty GTI has been designed for those who love the open road. The Hero is powerful but easy to handle. It comes in a range of fashionable colours. A soft-top convertible model is also available.

<u>The Leander</u>

An estate car that will suit all your needs. Whether you are stocking up at the supermarket or taking the family on holiday, you will have plenty of room in this spacious car. Petrol or diesel, manual or automatic, the Leander has a model for you.

<u>The Nile</u>

With this multi-purpose vehicle you can seat 8 comfortably and still find room for the luggage. The seats can be arranged in a variety of positions. Days out are great fun in a Nile.

Visit Wrighton Motors this weekend and see this unique collection for yourself.

T Exam Practice 4 Document 3

WRIGHTON MOTORS

If you are looking for a used car then visit our showrooms. We have a large range of used cars in all price ranges. We are sure you will find something to suit your needs. Buying from Wrighton Motors gives you the assurance that your new car will prove to be reliable and in top condition. All our used cars have a one-year warranty.

Below is a selection of the used cars we currently have on offer.

Car Details		Description	Special Offers*	
Make	Year		Trade Price**	Our Price
		Hatchbacks		
Pearl	J	Perfect as a run around, hatchbacks suit the smaller family or as a second car.	£4,500	£4,250
Chiltern	L		£5,000	£4,600
BWD 934	M		£5,400	£5,150
Fifi	P		£6,750	£6,525
Pearl	G		£3,200	£3,000
		Saloons		
Malvern	P	These family cars are excellent value. Many come with power-assisted steering, central locking and stereo radio/cassette.	£11,500	£11,200
Chloe	K		£ 7,500	£ 7,350
Sapphire	F		£ 5,500	£ 5,250
BWD 964	N		£ 9,500	£ 8,999
Chloe	D		£ 4,500	£ 4,000
		Estates		
Diamond	M	We have a large range of estate cars. Manual or automatic, these spacious vehicles are suitable for a variety of uses.	£14,000	£13,250
Buxton	K		£11,500	£11,200
Chantel	L		£12,999	£12,650
BDW 984	J		£ 9,999	£ 9,480
Diamond	H		£ 8,750	£ 8,500

* These special offers are for a limited period only.
** Trade prices quoted for January 1997.

T Exam Practice 4 Document 4

WRIGHTON MOTORS
Drake Street
PORTSMOUTH
PO9 8JK

Phone: 01823 2838822

Details Request Form

Make	Model	Price Range
UK MOTORS	MALVERN	£10,000 - £12,000
BEAUVAIS CARS	CHLOE	£ 8,000 - £ 9,500

Would you like to receive details of our interest-free finance deals?

Yes [X] No [ ]

I ~~would~~/would not like my name to be added to your mailing list*

Name MR DAVID HILL

Address 17 APSLEY ROAD, PORTSMOUTH

Postcode PO6 9ZZ

Telephone Number 01823 624491 Date (Date of typing)

* Delete as appropriate

COPIES MARTIN PETTY
FILE

COPIES MARTIN PETTY ✓
FILE

COPIES MARTIN PETTY
FILE ✓

Wrighton Motors
Drake Street
PORTSMOUTH
PO9 8JK